END TIME WARRIORS

JOHN KELLY
PAUL COSTA

PALM TREE
PUBLICATIONS
A Division Of
PALM TREE PRODUCTIONS

PUBLISHED BY PALM TREE PUBLICATIONS
A DIVISION OF PALM TREE PRODUCTIONS
HINESVILLE, GEORGIA, U.S.A.
PRINTED IN THE U.S.A.

Palm Tree Productions is a Media Services Company dedicated to seeing the Kingdom of God
advanced by ministries and businesses with excellence, integrity and professionalism through the
use of high quality media resources. Whether the publication is print, audio or visual, we are
dedicated to excellence in every aspect from concept to final production.

It is our desire that this publication will enrich your life and cause you to increase in wisdom and
understanding.

For more information about products and services available through Palm Tree Productions, visit
our website at www.palmtreeproductions.net.

Cover Design & Layout by Wendy K. Walters, Palm Tree Productions

LIBRARY OF CONGRESS CATALOGING-IN-PUBLICATION DATA
Kelly, John, 1943–
        End time warriors / John Kelly, with Paul Costa.
            p.   cm.
        ISBN 0-9787128-0-3
        1. Church renewal Miscellanea. 2. Private revelations.
        I. Costa, Paul, 1941–   . II. Title.
        BV600.2.K4125   1999   99-39947
        269—dc21
        CIP

Rights for publishing this book in other languages are contracted by LEAD.
www.leadtoachieve.com

CONTENTS

THE
TIME TO
ARISE

Throughout this decade, I have had the joy of encouraging individuals around the world to pray to the "Lord of the Harvest" to raise up harvesters *now* and in the next generation. As director of the World Prayer Center in Colorado Springs, I am always looking for key revelation that will encourage the Body of Christ in the midst of the chaotic, changing times we are in worldwide. *End Time Warriors* fulfills this requirement.

At this historic millennial shift, change and conflict abound throughout the earth at an accelerated pace. The world changes so quickly each day that many awaken with anxiety. We find ourselves groping for stability, footing and positioning. Our societal institutions change at a rapid pace from region to region—the entire earth seems to be in a constant state of earthquake.

It is also a time of great conflict. Another word for conflict is "warfare," a clash with an enemy (of tangible nature or imagined perception). However, God, the omnipotent Creator, has always had a remnant leadership that arises in the midst of conflict. He activates their faith and determines the course of events; He molds the world for generations to come.

God has a priesthood, a nation above all nations, that He draws near to Him and communicates His kingdom desires to so that His victory goes forth on the earth. He then says to this priesthood of believers, called the Church: "Rise up and war until you see My purposes for this generation established!" In *End Time Warriors*, apostle John Kelly declares to the Body of Christ: "Now is that time to arise!"

The Body of Christ is being prepared to approach the next millennium with an overcoming spirit and mentality. When I first met John Kelly, I knew I had met a leader, someone who understood war, and most of all, someone who knew the General of the Army to which I reported. To be victorious in any army, one must understand authority. In the Bible, there is the story of the Roman centurion, another soldier, who understood the nature of authority so well that Jesus said of him, "I tell you the truth, I have not found anyone in Israel with such great faith" (Matt. 8:10). By understanding the principles of authority in this book, you will find your faith being increased as you read—faith that can be as deep as the Roman centurion's.

This book will cause leaders to review how they are building the Kingdom. When the Lord ascended, He gave gifts to men so that His Church could be built. To build means to add sons and daughters until the house and inheritance of the future is secure. I have never read a more vivid account of how and why we build. There is a biblical pattern for establishing the Church of which the gates of hell cannot prevail.

This is a book of order. In the Word of God, we find that God is not only the Creator of all, but He has a sequence of events in His creative mind that establishes victory and success in us on earth. In 1 Corinthians 12:28, we find "first apostles." The word "first" means a prototype. John Kelly understands this order and communicates the importance of apostolic authority for the end-time battle. In this same verse, we find "second prophets." Without prophetic insight, vision and revelatory understanding, we do not advance, but retreat. This book releases vision and understanding for advancement of the Kingdom.

Finally, this is a book of harvest. With principles of multiplication and admonishment against waste, we can advance the Kingdom with a mentality of success instead of selfishness and poverty. The call to unity that our Lord extended to the Body of Christ prevails throughout the reading. I love this statement in John Kelly's vision that I feel communicates our Lord's heart in John 17:

> *Then everything stopped. Nothing else came to me in vision or dream. Then the Lord said to me, "I will not show you the rest, for that is for no man to know. There are men in my ministry who want a guarantee of the end time. They want to know beforehand what is going to happen. Tell them it is a battle, but there is a corporate anointing for the battle."*

I do not know of a book that has been written recently that will prepare our hearts with vision for things to come in the end as I have found in *End Time Warriors*.

CHUCK D. PIERCE

GOD'S CAMPAIGN

Your sons and daughters will prophesy, your old men will dream dreams, your young men will see visions. Even on my servants, both men and women, I will pour out my Spirit in those days.

JOEL 2:28,29

The Bible tells us that in the last days our young men will see visions and our old men will dream dreams. By these standards, I've come to the conclusion that I must be middle-aged. Frankly, I enjoy being middle-aged and having both dreams and visions.

In 1996, God gave me a series of dreams and visions over a three-month period that began when my wife and I were praying and interceding for other ministries. The dreams and visions usually took place on ministerial trips as I slept or in the privacy of my bedroom (which is where I do most of my praying) both alone and with my wife.

The content of these visions is significant. I feel that I must share it. I confess that these dreams and visions were fragmented and impossible to comprehend in the natural realm. However, in October of 1996, as I was taking a nap just hours before I was to speak at our annual Men in Ministry Conference of Antioch Churches & Ministries (ACM), I awoke with three dreams flooding into my mind. Then the Lord spoke to me:

> When you get up to speak tonight, I want you to speak under My spirit of prophecy. The dreams and visions that I have given you will come together.

I trusted God that He would give me the prophetic unction and call and that I would give the interpretation in the form of a prophetic utterance. I scrapped the message I had prepared, for I knew I had to give what God had commanded me to give. The Lord blessed me as I gave His message that night, and it came out in logical sequence and made perfect sense.

What God showed me was a victorious group of warriors. They were from all generations past, since the beginning of time. What really amazed me was that the strongest warriors were the present-day warriors; they were much bigger and stronger (spiritually) than even the Christians of biblical times. These young warriors had received the sum total of past and present truth and the past and present moves of God, so that there was tremendous increase in knowledge and impartation by the Spirit. They had become strong by being properly discipled in the house of God (the Church)—nurtured by the mothers of Israel and patriarchs who poured their lives into them.

Present-day warriors have the advantage of all the things that God has done and revealed throughout history, and consequently, are stronger than even our forefathers of the faith. I saw the faces and the size of these warriors, and with each generation they were larger. They were all on the earth at the same time; I found that awesome!

I'm considered to be what is called a "high-D personality," a-goal-a-day-keeps-the-doctor-away type of fellow. I have to have a mission, a cause, a fate or a responsibility to perform. One of the things I saw in the dream was that the Army of God was constantly going into valleys and mountains, but the enemy was always on the other side of the hill. The Army of God never went directly over the hill and into the enemy camp until my later visions. Just the thought that the enemy was on the other side of the hill and was not being attacked I found very frustrating, let alone upsetting, because when it comes to the enemy, the Army of God must be the aggressor. Not to engage the enemy while thinking we are engaging the enemy is a very frustrating proposition.

I heard the Army of God blowing trumpets. I saw them go from a mode of praise and worship to a mode of battle preparation. Sadly, I saw the Army of God waste the anointing He had given them. I could see that the oil of God was coming forth from the bellies of the warriors, but as the Living Water came forth, it simply fell upon the ground. This water was supposed to be aimed at the demonic forces, but it was not. However, later in my vision I could see Living Water coming out of stronger warriors (the new breed), and when it struck the demons, they melted, dissipated, and formed a puddle on the ground.

The Lord showed me the many-colored uniforms of the Army of God, and how it has to be a multipurpose, multifaceted army. It wasn't good to camp around one doctrine or one move of the Spirit, for His Army had to embrace all that God had revealed in past and present truth, and past and present moves of His Spirit.

To be balanced is not to have a little bit of this and a little bit of that. It is to be radical about everything that God's Word says and to embrace it all. I like to refer to myself as being a Presbyterian because I believe in the plurality of elders; I'm Episcopalian because I believe in the authority of the bishops; I'm Methodist because I believe in small-group dynamics; I'm Baptist because I believe in baptism by immersion; I'm Pentecostal because I believe in speaking in tongues; I'm Mennonite because I believe in the community life of the Saints, etc. In the same way we need to embrace the various Charismatic moves of the Spirit: word of faith, healing, deliverance, Latter Rain movement, Manifest Sons movement, Revival movement, church restoration movement, the restoration of church government movement, etc.

God expects His ministers to be a fighting force. In order to become a strong fighting unit, we must establish covenant relationships with each other. Ministers have to be willing to make the same kind of commitment as an 18-year-old heathen who has joined the military. When an 18-year-old unbeliever joins the Army, Navy, Air Force, Coast Guard or Marines, he has committed himself to the overall vision of the military—protecting his nation. He is committed to the fact that he is under orders from the President himself (in our case it would be the Lord). He is committed to not breaking relationship with the military force that he has joined.

The dreams and visions that God showed me had an incredible effect on me. I realized my frailty as a minister and began to wonder if I was doing some things for my benefit, fame and glory rather than wanting my spiritual sons and daughters to be successful. I began to realize that many great and good men and women of God were wasting themselves on vain efforts and were measuring success based on how many books and tapes they sold, how many conferences they preached at, which big churches they preached in, how many thousands of Christians they preached to, how much money came into their ministries, how much money they were making, etc. None of those should be our measure of success. Our success should be measured by the quality of the sons and daughters whom we are preparing for building the kingdom of God. Do they have God's vision? Are they determined in wanting to see God's vision come to fruition on the earth (see Matt. 11:12)? Are they willing to be prophetic and to take a prophetic stand? Are they willing to take a principled stand? Do they have a balance between character and charisma? Do they understand the greatness of a corporate anointing versus an individual anointing? Are they committed to each other's success just as we, the spiritual fathers, should be committed to their success? These visions have moved me to commit myself to building greater houses and nurturing disciples who will do greater works than I have done.

We must not keep our spiritual sons and daughters in bondage to our vision. They must be allowed to pursue and build the houses (churches and/or ministries) God has called them to. We are building churches according to man-made patterns and creating pyramidal, hierarchical systems. What happens is that our sons and daughters cannot rise above this system and establish their own houses.

I am beginning to understand my own mortality. The older I get, the more I get tired of playing church. The older I get, the more I find that I want to take a stand against the injustices and the sins of society. The older I get, the more ferocious I feel about taking on the enemy. Is seeing my picture on a magazine cover going to be important? Is the size of my bank account going to be important? How many years do I have left to give my life for the sake of the gospel, and what is going to be important to me?

In my early ministry I gave myself to the making of disciples, raising up of elders and raising up of set-men (men who are the head of a ministry), but now I find myself wanting to pour myself into the young apostles. My concern is for apostles—in particular those who act as apostolic Lone Rangers—who could be greatly synergized if they were part of a team of apostles. They would still have opportunities to build their own networks, but their networks would have a greater degree of balance. Instead of being just evangelistic, prophetic, teacher-oriented or world-missions oriented, these apostles could covenant with other networks and be radical about everything in God's Word.

At first I could not comprehend the dreams and visions the Lord had given me. Just as Joshua had no comprehension that he was speaking to the Commander of the Lord of Hosts at Jericho (see Josh. 5:13,14), and Nebuchadnezzar had no comprehension of who the fourth man was in the fiery furnace (see Dan. 3:24,25), neither did I understand the visions clearly. It wasn't until I had given it as a prophetic address to the men at our Men in Ministry Conference that I realized the great Warrior who had spoken to me was that same Warrior who was in the fiery furnace and the same One who confronted Joshua at Jericho.

I'm a rather large man in size and height, but this heavenly Warrior seemed at least four feet taller than me, and much broader and wider. Actually he reminded me of a time in Orlando when I came walking around a corner in a mall and literally bumped into Shaquille O'Neal. I'm 6' 3," but when I bumped into O'Neal all I remember is looking straight into his diaphragm. I felt like a child. The difference in our size created the impression of an older, mature man walking with a little kid.

I began to realize that the warrior messenger I encountered may have actually been a Christophany, which is the Lord Himself in the form of a man. The whole time in I conversed with the Warrior, I felt childlike and immature. I felt like a little boy who was being led by the hand of his father or by some great hero and was being shown all the wonders of a museum. Yet initially, I didn't think of the figure as the Lord. I never contextualized the visions and dreams until I was speaking and it wasn't until the very end that the impact of the Warrior's identity hit me. This was the Lord Himself and not just an angel.

What follows in this book is a mosaic of three dreams and three visions that I received over a three-month period. God gave me these dreams and visions in multiples of three, which I believe is significant, because God often does the important things in multiples of three: the Trinity; the body, soul and spirit of man; the outer court, the inner court and the holy of holies of the Tabernacle, etc.

After I had the last dream, I was able to put the revelations together and have a clear understanding of what God was trying to tell me. God was revealing to me the present condition of the Church. He was giving me an end-time warfare strategy for His Body. This book reveals the battle plan—a war we can and will win.

JOHN KELLY

CHAPTER ONE

THE VISION

SEEING THE NATURE OF THE WAR

As the vision began, I was walking in a field where the grass was not very high. There I saw lush, green hills and felt a refreshing, cooling breeze touching my face. Then I felt the Lord lift me up.

As I was being lifted into the air, I looked over to my right where I could see a field glistening with gold. A figure appeared before me. I couldn't quite make him out, but it gradually became clear to me that it was the Lord, dressed in the fashion of a mighty warrior. The Warrior spoke to me and said, "That is the field ripe for harvest, and what is glistening gold in your eyes are souls."

Then the Warrior said, "Now I will take you to that field ripe for harvest." But when he took me to the field, there was nothing there. I could see only fire and smoke in the clouds hovering over the field.

I asked, "What is going on here?"

The Warrior said to me, "Underneath the clouds where the battle is raging, there is the field ripe for harvest." He paused, and then said, "Things are happening here in the air."

THE BATTLE LINE

I looked to my left, beyond an open field to a series of valleys. In the first valley there gathered a huge fighting force of warriors with all kinds of armament and in all kinds of battle gear ranging from ancient to modern. The Lord took me closer, and I could see that the warriors were, in fact, small, hideous demons wearing uniforms.

Then He said, "This is the battle line."

Then the Lord took me over the hill and into the next valley where I saw battalions so numerous I couldn't count them. The Lord said, "Each of these battalions represents men and women in My ministry."

Each battalion had a banner, and that banner was their identification. It was who they were; it was the banner they fought under. There was the discipleship banner, the faith banner, the deliverance banner, the holiness banner, the Calvinist banner, the charismatic banner, the shepherding banner, the Pentecostal banner and so forth. The battalions were groups and denominations in existence in the evangelical Church today.

Off in the distance, I could see a very small battalion, but I could not see it clearly.

MINISTERING IN PRECISION

The Warrior said to me, "Do you want to have some fun?"

"Yes," I said, perhaps a bit tentatively.

"Watch this."

The Warrior blew His trumpet, and all the Lord's troops rose from their camps and marched into the field. They swarmed over the hill, heading toward the enemy camp, but before they reached the battle line, they all stopped.

Each battalion then formed a circle and began to walk in precision. One of the battalions was very precise. Another battalion was holding hands and dancing. Other battalions danced in various ways, turning and twisting to music only they could hear. Other battalions just stood in their circles, but all the battalions were in this formation.

The little group that was over by itself didn't even respond to the sound of the trumpet. It was as if they never heard it. I assumed that these men had no ears to discern what the trumpet was saying.

Meanwhile the enemy soldiers had come out of their camp and were waiting for God's Army to engage them in battle. When the Army of God formed their circles, showing no signs of engaging the enemy, the little enemy warriors went to the battalions of the Army of God and began to pelt them with small daggers, arrows, sticks and stones. The demons cursed and laughed at them, mocking the Lord's Army. Three enemy platoons surrounded the circles that the Army of God had formed.

From the midst of the fray, I could hear the soldiers of God screaming, "We're at war! We're at war! This is war! We are the Army of God!"

At first it was thrilling to see the Army of God on the battlefield with their corporate anointing. Then the Warrior brought me closer and I could see the enemy mocking them.

Then the Army of God turned around and went back to the valley they had come from.

SPILLING THE INCORRUPTIBLE SEED

I apologize if this part of the vision offends some readers because this is not my intention. This vision is merely a word picture of what is going on in the Church today and it is central to what God has shown me. Later in the book, I will attempt to explain the sin of Onan as mentioned in Scripture, Genesis 38:8-10. The truths in this segment are applicable to both men and women though the content is set in a male orientation.

What I saw next horrified me. I said, "No, this vision is not of God. I rebuke it in the name of Jesus!" The vision then stopped. This happened one night as I was in prayer.

On another night I had the same dream. I was in the same place as in the first dream and I saw the same vile happenings. Again I said, "I rebuke this in the name of Jesus. This dream is not of God."

Repeatedly the Warrior said to me, "You will speak this at Men in Ministry." He wanted me to share this vision at our upcoming men's conference.

I was later given the same dream and vision but as I was about to rebuke it, a voice said to me, "If you rebuke Me, the Lord your God, one more time, I will rebuke you! You will speak of this vision!"

I was appalled at what I saw then! The men from the battalions had formed circles, and they were spilling their seed on the ground.

I said, "God, what is this foul, lustful, sexual thing I am seeing?"

God said, "It is none of that. Get your mind out of that place; that's not what I am talking about. What you see are men and women in ministry wasting the seed of My anointing by not producing spiritual sons and daughters. Yes, they preach, prophesy and exercise spiritual gifts over My people, but they are not building into My people. They are wasteful! Doesn't the Word speak of My incorruptible seed and the corruptible seed? What I am showing you is that My incorruptible seed can be corrupted by the wasteful use and dissipation of My anointing."

As I looked again, the people in the circles were cheering about how far certain individuals could cast their seed.

VANITY OF THE FLESH

Now the Lord blew His trumpet and the Army of God got up and went back to their encampment. Then the Lord said to me, "Now, listen."

The soldiers were exclaiming to one another, "Man, we were attacked! We've been persecuted. What opposition! What warfare! We were tearing down strongholds. Now we can go have a breakthrough conference. Everyone will be changed from now on." And they began organizing breakthrough meetings and celebrating a victory such as had never before happened.

The people thought they had been on the battlefield, but they never had been.

The Warrior said, "They are mocked because of the vanity of their flesh and they interpret that as persecution."

I fell to my knees, saying, "God, I repent! I repent!"

GO TO THE CROSS

Speaking of the men spilling their seed, the Lord said to me, "My son, they know not what they do. Take your criticism and put it at the foot of the Cross, and you weep for these men. Cry for these men. Have compassion for these men. Have mercy for these men."

The Lord continued, "This is a warning against mixing with nonvirile, nonproducing breeds; it is a warning against mixing incorruptible seed with corruptible seed. This is a warning for all the battalions in My kingdom."

JUST BUILDING HOUSES

I said to the Lord, "At least those ministers made an effort. When the trumpet blew, they went over the hill."

The Warrior rebuked me, saying, "Are you thinking of the small group in the distance?"

"Yes, when you blew the trumpet, that small group never moved."

The Warrior said, "Would you like to see what they were doing?"

"Certainly," I said, "because I would like to preach against that kind of behavior." So the Lord took me to where the small group was waiting.

The Warrior said, "Watch!" He blew the trumpet and the small group never moved. Suddenly they turned and went backward.

I said, "I can't believe it; they're retreating on the day of battle!"

In fact, the group had set about building houses. At least the other groups had made an effort to go to war; this group was content to construct houses.

HOW ARE WE BUILDING?

The Warrior said to me, "Watch this!" He blew the trumpet and out of the houses came young warriors. Again He blew the trumpet and the young warriors turned around and built houses themselves.

Again He blew the trumpet, and out of the new houses came younger warriors. He blew the trumpet again, and the younger warriors built houses. He blew the trumpet again, and out of the houses came even younger warriors.

Then He said, "Come back with Me as I blow the trumpet again."

Frustrated, I said, "Wait a minute, Warrior, what's wrong with these ministers? When the trumpet blows they turn around and build houses."

"They are properly discerning the sound of the trumpet," the Warrior explained. "For they are building My habitation. They are building My house. Shall we go back there again since you did not properly discern this yourself?" He asked.

"Yes," I said, chagrined.

TRAINING IN THE HOUSE

The Warrior took me back to see the small group again, and I was amazed at what I saw! The young warriors were larger, more muscular and more fierce looking than the older warriors. In fact, each generation of warriors was more muscular and fierce than the generation before them.

I was about to ask how the warriors got so strong, but the Lord knew the question I was about to ask. He said, "Because each one works out harder in the house where he trains."

At this point I knew that the Warrior who had been showing me these things was indeed the Lord.

ATTACKING SEPARATELY

The Lord said to me, "Are you ready to see the corporate anointing on the day of battle?"

I said, "Yes, Lord, I'm ready to see the corporate anointing on the day of battle!"

The trumpet sounded a long, loud call. All the troops moved out of their camps and went to the top of the hill. There they stopped.

The Lord said, "Look at them!"

I could see that each group carried a different banner and wore a different-colored uniform from other groups. The Army of God was once again preparing to attack the enemy.

The Lord said, "This group is going to attack them through faith. This group is going to attack them through discipline. This group is going to attack them through deliverance. This group will attack through personal ministry. That is the prophetic battalion. That is the evangelist."

THE REMNANT ARMY OF GOD

The Lord said, "Let us go and inspect that small group."

I went with Him to see the small group. They were not in a group like the other battalions I had seen, but were arrayed in rows. Nor did they all wear the same uniform. In the first row there were men in the discipleship uniform, the holiness uniform, Pentecostal uniform, charismatic uniform, faith uniform—every kind of uniform that you could imagine.

I said, "They look like a ragtag militia."

The Lord said, "These are My special troopers. They were seen as misfits when they were in the larger battalions. Their vision went beyond what My Church accepts as normal. They were misfits because they had something stirring within them; they could not tolerate standing around in circles spilling their seed. Look at the uniforms of the troops behind them."

When I looked beyond the first row, I could see that the remainder of the troops wore uniforms of many colors, much like the mental image I have always had of Joseph's coat of many colors. The collars of their uniforms were made up of every color. The soldiers represented every race, every ethnic group, every theological persuasion.

I asked, "Why have they stopped here?"

The Lord said, "Because they are surveying the battlefield."

FAILING FAITH

From where the armies of hell were gathered for battle, I could hear the fierce screaming of the demons. From among the Army of God, a large battalion named Faith began approaching the armies of hell, but they turned back because they had no faith. They kept believing that the battlefield would change, but it did not. The armies of hell remained fierce and intimidating.

The Army of God launched an assault on the enemy camp, while Faith trailed behind. The small group had yet to move. A great slaughter was taking place on the battlefield; the Army of God was being defeated by the enemy.

Then I saw the small group begin to form a wedge.

THE WEDGE

"What are they doing?" I asked.

The Lord said, "This is the wisdom that was given to Moses. Some have said it is an elitist principle, some call it hierarchy, but to form a wedge is a tactic of warfare. The captains over thousands are going first, not last."

The captains were at the front of the wedge, and I could see that every generation behind formed a new wedge. (There were actually four wedges in all.) The battle raged with new intensity as the wedge entered the enemy camp. The second wedge was even more aggressive than the first. They were literally pushing the older warriors through the battlefield. The older warriors were strong enough to do the fighting, but the force of the ministers behind them was such that the first wedge was powerfully driven through the heart of the enemy's camp.

Finally they broke through and surrounded the entire enemy army. The Army of God began to slaughter them; blood was running in the field. Then, suddenly, God's warriors, both old and young, began running to the field I had seen at the beginning of the vision — the field where there was smoke and fire.

PRAYER WARRIORS

Suddenly the sky was filled with objects flying overhead. These things were coming from the houses that I had seen being built. I realized that these flying objects were in fact the prayers of the saints, who were doing spiritual warfare and tearing down powers and principalities.

Down on the field where there was fire and smoke, warriors who were evangelists went into the field. There they began reaching under the fire and smoke and pulling out golden souls. As they were doing this, baskets of golden souls began to form in the midst of the battlefield. A line of these baskets formed, leading all the way back to the houses which had been built.

Some men came running out from the midst of the battle. At first I thought they were cowards, but the Lord said, "Those are My platoons of pastors going back to gather the harvest into My house and raise up generation after generation until I come."

FOUNDATIONS APPEAR

Then I saw apostles and prophets in the harvest field, on the battlefield and back at the houses. The prophets were prophesying and the parts of the Body began coming together. The apostles were giving strategies and tactics. I could see a mighty fighting force being formed and taking shape under the guidance of the apostles. A harvest was taking place and, simultaneously, the harvest was being formed into a fighting force.

Show Us!

Then everything stopped. Nothing else came to me in vision or dream. Then the Lord said to me, "I will not show you the rest because that is for no man to know. There are men in My ministry who want a guarantee of the end time. They want to know beforehand what is going to happen. Tell them it is a battle, but there is a corporate anointing for the battle."

The Lord showed me that the other group was also anointed—the group which had been so easily defeated by the enemy. "Theirs was an individual anointing," He said, "and it was every man for himself on the battlefield. Because these lacked the corporate anointing, when one warrior was attacked, there were no other warriors there to help him fend off the enemy. They were not fighting back-to-back!

"However, when one has the corporate anointing and the enemy attacks, it is like they are attacking all of My Army. Victory will not come through the ferocity of a single warrior, but through the ferocity of the brothers and sisters who join him in battle."

CHAPTER TWO

DECEPTIVE ENEMY TACTICS

DISCERNING FIELDS RIPE FOR HARVEST

I was walking in a field where the grass was not very high. There I saw lush, green hills and felt a refreshing, cooling breeze touching my face. Then I felt the Lord lift me up.

As I was being lifted into the air, I looked over to my right where I could see a field glistening with gold. A figure appeared before me. I couldn't quite make Him out, but it gradually became clear to me that it was the Lord, dressed in the fashion of a mighty warrior. The Warrior spoke to me and said, "That is the field ripe for harvest, and what is glistening gold in your eyes are souls."

Then the Warrior said, "Now I will take you to that field ripe for harvest." But when He took me to the field, there was nothing there. I could see only fire and smoke in the clouds hov-

ering over the field.

I asked, "What is going on here?"

The Warrior said to me, "Underneath the clouds where the battle is raging, there is the field ripe for harvest." He paused, then said, "Things are happening here in the air."

At first glance, the glistening, golden field appeared to be an easy harvest, but the appearance was deceptive. In reality, the field was heavily guarded by the enemy.

When I came closer I discovered a raging battle in the field that was swirling in fire and smoke. This is a classic maneuver by the enemy—a trick of Satan—to let it *appear* that there is an easy harvest, ripe and ready to be gleaned. What is waiting is the enemy's resistance. The Church goes in unprepared, without a strategy or plan, and they come away with little results and discouraged because they did not take into account the enemy barring their way.

FAILED VISIONS

The harvest that appears to be ready but isn't, represents a failed vision. Many bona fide visions from God result in failure because the servants given such revelations encounter spiritual resistance and fail to achieve what God desires. How many times have we heard, "God said I am to do this..." only to find out months or years later that the vision failed because the soldiers given the command failed to carry through the Lord's objective?

VISIONS ARE AFFECTED BY EMOTIONAL DYSFUNCTION AND MANIPULATION

Many "visions" come out of emotional dysfunction in a person's heart. Christians who hunger for a lot of attention come up with attention-getting visions that are often revelations rooted in various insecurities and fears.

These paranoias influence us in determining the direction God is going. So when we see the field ripe for harvest—a genuine vision—we miss God because we are influenced by so many other factors. Apostolic missionary Terry King, who has served as a pastor and foreign missionary for years, says:

> I define manipulation as a crafty and coercive means to get others to do our bidding. It seems to me that, in most cases, the temptation to manipulate comes from our own insecurities. Why is it that the ministry seems to draw such insecure men? I think the answer may be that we are all insecure. Men are insecure. It's part of the curse, I believe, that we've got to overcome in Christ. But it does seem that the ministry does draw particularly insecure men. We have learned to cover up that insecurity with all kinds of things. It seems that one of the things is manipulation, coercing, or obligating people into doing the kind of things we want done, so that we feel like we're leading. It seems to me that this is not leadership at all.

FALSE AND FLATTERING VISIONS

Ezekiel 12:24 says, "For there will be no more false visions or flattering divinations among the people of Israel." There are true and legitimate visions and there are the false and flattering visions (divinations) too. If you don't understand God's vision, you are susceptible to the vain imaginations of other people (see Jer. 23:16,32).

False and flattering visions are sometimes the desire of man's heart (see Jer. 14:14). Our flesh cries out to be recognized and esteemed: "Give me your money and I will win the world to

MANY

SINCERE

LEADERS OF GOD

STRUGGLE

AGAINST THE

ATTRACTIVENESS

OF FALSE

AND

FLATTERING

VISIONS.

Christ for you." How many times have
we heard that on TV? I don't care how
big a group or a person gets, he still only
represents one part of what God is doing
throughout the world. The best we can
do is to join our brothers and sisters
around the world in winning the world
for Christ.

A false or flattering vision will always
thrust a Christian or an entire church
right into the midst of temptation. False
and flattering visions are tempting every
one of us. I believe many sincere leaders
of God struggle against the attractiveness
of false and flattering visions. The greater
the success in ministry, the greater the
temptation to think, *I'm God's chosen
instrument.* As in the vision, we see the
field, ripe with harvest and immediately
think, *This is mine. God has given this to
me. I must build a structure to contain it;
I must immediately influence all I can to
work toward building what God has shown
me.*

Some of the visions we hear about
are incredible! We hear about ministers
saying if they didn't build a particular
building, God was going to step on them
and kill them. I know someone who said
that God told him to build a hospital, but
a few months after he built it, he sold it.
You really have to scratch your head at

some of these things.

The reason we don't understand the purpose of God is because we don't understand the vision of God. We don't understand what He is looking for, or what He wants to see when He returns. He won't be looking for the fulfilled vision of a big white church on a hill. He'll be looking for a Bride that has been busily about His work—building His Kingdom.

THE "ONE-MAN SHOW"

Any dynamic leader can have a vision, but is that vision from God? These "one man shows" have ignited dramatic catastrophes in the past:

Jim Jones:
He started out as a Pentecostal minister and was ordained by a major Pentecostal denomination. At some point, he crossed over the line. He got away from the Bible, formulating his own doctrine and teaching. Through his charismatic personality many were fooled, thinking it was the anointing of God; instead it was a demonic anointing. He had false and flattering visions, but the visions were cosmic foolishness. The end was a disaster when this cult leader forced his followers and himself to drink poisoned Kool-Aid. The TV news showed the dead, bloated bodies of his followers—men, women and children—lying side by side in some field in Guyana.[1]

David Koresh:
Made the leader of the Branch Davidians in 1990, this self-proclaimed messiah eventually brought dozens of his followers to a horrific end three years later. Dozens were massacred by federal troops during a 51-day siege of the

religious leader's compound in Waco, Texas. Koresh, known for memorizing vast portions of the Bible, was able to deceive people.[2]

Marshal Applegate and the Heaven's Gate Cult:
This cult brought about the death of 39 men and women in San Diego, California. They died believing the most outrageous lie—that a spaceship was waiting to pick them up.[3]

In each of these instances the devil scoffed at Christians and many unbelievers mocked the faith. No doubt they all thought, *See what happens when you become too religious.* All of these one-man shows had the appearance of Christianity, but each leader and group was far from God's true kingdom.

Carnal religious leaders with strong manipulative personalities and visions are very dangerous. They may even preach the gospel, but they aren't true to the faith. Some leaders may even have some measure of a Christian heritage—Jim Jones and David Koresh were both preachers and Marshal Applegate was the son of a preacher—but they're far off the mark (see Titus 1:10,11; Jude 3,4).

ULTIMATE VISION

How do we stay on course for God's kingdom? Is there a way for us not to be lulled into false and flattering visions, building our own kingdoms or being a one-man show? There is a way.

Building the Kingdom in preparation for the coming of Christ is the compass that keeps us all moving in the same direction. This compass is vital. Every Christian should have the same ultimate vision of building the Kingdom in preparation for the second coming of Christ (see Matt. 6:33). All other visions are secondary to this ultimate goal and those visions include planting churches, missionary work, evangelistic crusades, Sunday

Schools, etc.

While speaking at a ministers' conference, I asked the men to close their eyes, raise their right hands and with their index fingers point to whatever direction they thought was due north. I asked the men to do this exercise until everyone had made a commitment to point in the direction they perceived to be north. When they finally opened their eyes, there was an outburst of laughter, because fingers were pointing in every imaginable direction. In the whole auditorium only a few men had identified the right direction.

Why did I do this? I wanted to show how easy it is to miss the true direction when we are not sensitive to our surroundings. When we are led by the flesh, we don't have a compass and we miss the vision. Even today, many of us in the charismatic movement have been so caught up in every whim of revelatory teaching that we have missed God's ultimate direction—Kingdom building. Sadly, the Church looks like many of those men who tried to identify due north, but ended up pointing in different directions.

90/10 PRINCIPLE

The Church needs Kingdom builders. The Church has gone long enough operating on the 90/10 principle, in which 10 percent are doing all the work and 90 percent are spectators. In professional ministry there is a distinction between clergy and laity. The root word for laity might as well be "laid back." Too often the word refers to the laid-back ones, the do-nothings or the slackers. It is abundantly clear that in Spirit-filled groups, we have too many who have a laid-back concept of "laity."

Taking cities for the Lord will not be done by men who are looking for a job or worried about their congregation, but by men who have a heart, anointing and calling to take a city. Taking a city has little to do with the person's preaching or teaching, but a whole lot to do with his ability to lead. The ability to lead is perhaps the most overlooked quality in the Body of Christ today, but it is one of the most important. One needs to lead by example – not by being a talking head to the congregation. We can only impart what we are; a poor leader will not get much done.

LEARNING BUT NOT DOING

Once I was in a church where the elders prophesied over everyone in the congregation every Sunday. There was a tremendous prophetic anointing in this place, but I have to wonder what the church would do if it grew to over a thousand people. Unless those Christians are trained, encouraged and nurtured to *do ministry individually and corporately*, a church will have problems growing. The question that should stir all of us is: *Are we merely learning and not doing?*

A church may have a great evangelistic anointing where people are being saved every Sunday. It's always great to see people coming to Christ, but you have to wonder if every other Sunday the back row is being lost. You may have a pastor who is a great teacher of the Word. You may see everybody prepared for Sunday service with pens and notebooks, too. But the crucial question again is: *Are we always learning but never doing?*

The Church needs leaders who can inspire and teach how each of us can build God's kingdom. Apostolic leadership is critical here. It takes apostolic leadership to build a big church; without this leadership affecting church elders, the local congregation will not be effective in the community.

APOSTLES DEMAND STRONG LEADERSHIP

An apostolic leader will bring true leadership to the church. He will demand leadership out of the fivefold ministries (i.e. apostle, prophet, evangelist, pastor and teacher); then they can take their city. It doesn't matter what a person's gift is. He will be able to raise up a large church if he is a strong leader.

When I was a young minister, I was ordained by two denominations, but I felt very alone and without real fellowship. I was at a meeting where the guest speaker was a very famous preacher. I thought if I could just have a few moments with this man, he could answer some of the questions I had about moving and ministering in the Spirit. After the meeting I had an opportunity. A pastor and I approached him and asked him for his advice. He said to us, "Always carry your briefcase with some papers in it. Put your money in a garbage bag, and place it behind the tire in the trunk of your car. That way, if robbers come, they will get the briefcase with the papers but not the money."

I can remember walking out of that meeting confused and deflated. But the next meeting I ministered at, I walked in with my garbage bag and briefcase. I thought if a preacher that popular and successful recommended something then there must be something to it. I was obviously wrong!

TEACH AND IMPART

At that time in my ministry, there was no one to impart anything to me. I have since discovered that, in order to fulfill a vision, there must be an impartation that multiplies growth and discipleship among God's people. These principles are in Ephesians 4:11-13:

> It was He who gave some to be apostles, some to be prophets, some to be evangelists, and some to be pastors and teachers, to prepare God's people for works of service, so that the body of Christ may be built up until we all reach unity in the faith and in the knowledge of the Son of God.

The multiplying effect comes when you teach and impart to others the ability to carry on the ministry.

GOD WANTS TO MULTIPLY

Our God is the God of multiplication. Pastors must prepare their people to be released to carry out their ministries across town or as missionaries in foreign fields. So many times we go to church and meet elders who are highly qualified to teach and preach, but they remain under the pastor, walking in the shadow of the pastor's vision. Often a pastor desires to keep these people working on his vision instead of releasing them to pursue their own visions in Christ. Sometimes a pastor will keep his good people so long that they will either break emotionally, or submit and surrender the vision God has given to them, or split away from the church in frustration.

The pastor may have a bona fide sub-vision—to build his church—but is he using others to build his sub-vision instead of having a releasing mentality, so the real vision of Kingdom building can be carried out? The vision of the glistening-gold field, ripe with harvest, can only be harvested if we multiply through impartation, relationship and networking.

Something good can be the enemy of God's best. A pastor can work hard, use God's gifting to strengthen and add members to a church. There is nothing wrong with that. Or a pastor can work hard, using God's gifting, and impart and develop men and women for the Kingdom—fellow ministers equipped for every good work and not merely spectators on the sideline—who can minister individually and corporately.

The pastor can plant people or churches using the same principle the farmer uses. When you plant one kernel of corn, at harvest time you will get around 1,200 kernels in return. When you plant 1,200 kernels of corn, you will harvest 1,440,000 kernels of corn. But if we eat the first harvest, then there is nothing to plant. God wants us to have the foresight to plant and multiply. He will not tolerate our eating what should be planted.

PLANTING IN MEXICO

Several years ago I went to Mexico City on a mission trip. I was there at the same time as another missionary group. The other group consisted of three missionaries and their wives; they were in Mexico City to plant a church.

While I was there I met with three Mexican pastors who were apostolic (they were builders). I told these men that we would train them and their leaders and show them how to plant churches. The Mexican pastors enthusiastically agreed. After several years these three Mexican pastors have planted over 150 churches with multiplied thousands attending services. The other group of three missionaries and their wives planted one church in Mexico City which has about 400 people. This group spent far more money than we did, but we were far more successful. Why? Because we used a biblical principle in planting and multiplication while they just added.

MISSED THE BOAT

Many people are caught up in popular Christianity and are not on the prophetic edge of what God is doing in the Church. Frankly, most of the Church has missed the boat, because they refuse to be part of what God is doing. However, He is going to do it anyway, whether we agree or not.

Since the Dark Ages, God has been progressively restoring the Church, and I believe that in the last 20 years the restoration has gone into high gear. God is a God of progress; He is always adding to us and doing something new.

God desires to bring revival and restoration to the Church,

and the reformation of cities and countries. However, the reformation of cities and countries cannot take place until there is revival and restoration in the Church. This is not just revival and restoration in the hearts of men and women, but it includes revival and restoration that will transform Church government and leadership.

The front lines of this war focus on the local church. If the local church is ineffective there will be no challenge to the enemy. On the other hand, if the local church is strengthened and learns to be discerning of the enemy's tactics, then it will become better equipped to reap the harvest. Yet, to be an effective fighting force, all believers must come to understand what God has taught us in how to fight the enemy. There are biblical patterns and truths we should follow if we expect to effectively overcome the enemy today.

NOTES
1. Michael Taylor, "Jones Captivated S.F.'s Liberal Elite." *San Francisco Chronicle,* (Nov. 12, 1998), n.p.; Michael Taylor, "Jonestown Suicides Shocked World." *Associated Press,* (March 27, 1997), n.p.; www.rickross.com. INTERNET.
2. Carol Moore, "Overview of the Davidian Massacre." Unknown source, (Dec. 1998), www.kreative.net/carolmoore/davidian-massacre, INTERNET.
3. Frank Bruni, "Cult Leader Believed in Space Aliens and Apocalypse" *New York Times* (March 28, 1997), n.p.; John Holliman, *Applewhite: From Young Overachiever to Cult Leader.* CNN, (March 28, 1997), www.rickross.com. INTERNET.

CHAPTER THREE

GOD'S BATTLE PLAN

BIBLICAL STRATEGIES FOR SUCCESS

*I looked to my left, beyond an open field, to a series of valleys.
In the first valley there gathered a huge fighting force of warriors with all kinds of armament and in all kinds of battle gear
ranging from ancient to modern. The Lord took me closer, and
I could see that the warriors were, in fact, small, hideous
demons wearing uniforms.*

Then He said, "This is the battle line."

The field in front of the demons was empty. I instantly realized
that the demonic forces were not being confronted by the Army
of God. The Lord's troops should have been pressing in and vio-
lently opposing the demonic forces, but God's Army couldn't be
seen because there was no clear-cut understanding of the practical

outworking of the Church. How could the Church, as a whole, confront the enemy when the Church, as a whole, did not understand its role, structure or government?

There are several things all believers must understand about our war against the enemy.

1. There are biblical patterns and structures for effective operation and use of leaders, gifts and resources.
2. A portion of our generated wealth should be consistently tithed to advance Kingdom endeavors.
3. Spiritual gifts should be used in the marketplace of the world to build financial resources for the Church.
4. A covenant of unity is critical for Christians to achieve victory against the enemy.

LEARNING TO WAGE WAR

Many years earlier the Lord had shown me the importance of His government in spiritual warfare. I was a traveling evangelist in those days and labored for the Lord mostly in the east. I was involved with preaching, faith healing and ministering deliverance to the oppressed. Everything seemed to be fine.

One day in Connecticut, as I was praying and seeking the Lord in a hotel room, I was stunned when the Lord said to me, "Your ministry is not in My Word!" I was shaken! I had just done a crusade for a group of five churches where over 100 people were saved. I had been part of God bringing healing and deliverance—young people were filled with the Holy Ghost. I preached from His Word, I ministered in the gifts from His Word (see 1 Cor. 12:7-11) and people were healed by His Word. Now the Lord of Glory declared that what I was doing was *not* in His Word!

With that jolting correction I began to search the Scriptures. I wanted my ministry to be *in* His word. Was there a godly pattern to follow? As I searched, I began to realize that most evangelists, prophets and trans-local ministries function in a pattern that is not from God. They don't have the slightest knowledge that God has a given a pattern for Church government and organization. Much of what is called "ministry" today isn't ministry at all! We call it ministry, but it's more the emulation of the music industry than the ministry of Christ – a maddening roadtrip of shows.

In those early years, much of what I did as a traveling evangelist (and much of what goes on today) was nothing more than a pep rally—a pep rally with preaching, healing, deliverance and salvation! People would say, "Oh, that was so good! I was so touched! Let's do this and that to the devil. Push 'im back, push 'im back, way back, shove 'im-back, shove 'im back! Rah, rah, rah!" Instead of raising up warriors in the Body, I was raising up cheerleaders in the Bride.

After being corrected by the Lord, I felt challenged to find the proper pattern in the Word. I searched the Word and sought the Lord for several months and the Lord began by showing me in the New Testament some insights into the fivefold ministry (apostle, prophet, evangelist, pastor and teacher as in Ephesians 4:11) and the raising up of spiritual fathers and sons. I began to understand the structure of the Church because God was giving me insight into the apostle, prophet and elder. Although I had a basic knowledge of the structure of Church government, I didn't understand the deeper theology, philosophy and life related to it.

THE PATTERN FOR CHURCH GOVERNMENT

God revealed to me how the Tabernacle is a type and shadow of the Church. The Israelites gave abundantly to the building of the

Tabernacle (see Exod. 35:20-29) as we should to the building up of the Church (see 2 Cor. 9:7).

He also showed me another type and shadow in the Old Testament, connected with diverting wealth to different kinds of storehouses. The Israelites channeled a measure of their prosperity to a village storehouse, city storehouse, and the storehouse of the king. These storerooms collected materials through a tithe that could be used to sustain the army and the inhabitants of a local town and village (see 1 Sam. 8:15-17; 1 Chron. 27:25; 2 Chron. 32:27,28).

All of these types and shadows—the Israelites using wealth to build the Tabernacle and tithing materials to local and royal storehouses—represented things to come. They are wise patterns for us today. Hebrews 8:5 speaks about building according to God's divine pattern. "See to it that you make everything according to the pattern shown you on the mountain." God said the same thing in the Old Testament. In Exodus 25:9, God explains, "Make this tabernacle and all its furnishings exactly like the pattern I will show you."

Throughout Scripture, particularly in Exodus, Numbers, Deuteronomy, Chronicles and Kings, there is support for this kind of organization. In the modern Church, every time there is a violation of this structure, the result is division in our ranks. We need to tithe and devote the appropriate resources to building the Church (a kind of Tabernacle for us today) by tithing to our local congregations (a kind of village storehouse), to the citywide church or ministry (a kind of city storehouse), and to large national and worldwide Church efforts (a kind of kingly storehouse). When used corporately, these resources advance the Kingdom everywhere.

There are those who don't understand this. There are elders and ministers I have met who don't understand the nature of consistent giving. I'm convinced it's because they don't want to understand. They can understand that the pastor should tithe, but they can't see why the Church—all believers—must tithe. It's because they don't understand the village and city concept. They don't understand that such giving is for their protection as God's kingdom is strengthened.

FINANCIAL RESOURCES ADVANCE THE KINGDOM

Years ago, the Lord focused my attention on tithing. I didn't understand why God was doing this, but my mind was stuck on Malachi 3:10, where it says, "Bring the whole tithe into the storehouse." I began to see God's structure for ministry was strongly connected to the proper role of tithing and channeling such tithe to the proper storehouses of the Church. Exodus 12:36 says:

> The LORD had made the Egyptians favorably disposed toward the people, and they gave them what they [the Israelites] asked for; so they plundered the Egyptians.

When the Israelites came out of captivity, they plundered the Egyptians and brought the fortunes with them. What is important to know is that this plunder later went to the building of the Tabernacle in the wilderness. The Israelites prioritized the use of their resources and devoted the wealth as offerings to build the Lord's Tabernacle.

In the same fashion, believers gain a measure of wealth from the secular world just as Isaiah 61:6 says:

> And you will be called priests of the Lord, you will be named ministers of our God. You will feed on the wealth of nations, and in their riches you will boast.

APPROPRIATE

GIVING

TO THE

BUILDING

OF

GOD'S

KINGDOM

MUST

ALWAYS

BE A

PRIORITY.

Like the Israelites we obtain by labor, opportunity, wisdom and inheritance a degree of wealth from living in this world, and like them we should have priorities as to where such wealth goes in building God's kingdom. The Church is a pattern and type of the Tabernacle for Christians, and we should prioritize our resources as the Israelites did. We need to diligently and consistently devote the wealth we gain to the building of His House.

Appropriate giving to the building of God's kingdom must always be a priority. It is the means by which the Army of God will prepare for war.

SPIRITUAL GIFTS GARNER WEALTH

We must use our spiritual gifts (see 1 Cor. 12:7-11; Rom. 12:4-8) and natural abilities among unbelievers for the purpose of gaining wealth that can be devoted to building the Kingdom. When financial and physical wealth is created, God calls us to appropriately tithe to the storehouses in the village, to the city and to the king's holding. Using our gifts in the marketplace can be quite intimidating, but the results are tremendous for the local church, an entire community of churches and for the Church in the heart of an entire nation.

But it isn't easy to use your gift in the world to advance God's kingdom. For instance, it's easy to prophesy in church where there's an atmosphere for it. The real test is in the secular marketplace among the demons. We need to have the courage to use our gifts outside church walls.

Several years ago, I was walking out of the Air Club in the Charlotte Airport when I noticed Jesse Jackson walking in front of me. I was minding my own business, when the Spirit of God said to me, "Prophesy." For several moments I wrestled with God as He nudged me to speak to this influential American. Finally I gave in to His prompting and used the gift He had given to me to speak. The first thing out of my mouth was, "Jesse."

He answered, "Hi!"

I said, "Why do you think so lowly of your race that you don't believe they can overcome?"

The reporters snapping his picture and trying to interview him all of a sudden moved away, making a path between him and me. Everyone within earshot stopped, and a hush fell over the crowd. There was a large black man standing nearby. I don't know who he was, but he said, "Hear this, hear this everybody. I want all of you to hear this!"

With that introduction, I gave a difficult prophetic word that challenged many of the ideas Jackson had on drugs, illicit sex and abortion. Still, I spoke as the Lord led, and it was one of the greatest prophecies that I ever gave, because it was spoken among many unbelievers and not in a church atmosphere where prophesying is easy.

Having the courage to use our gifts in the world is the first step, but we should also use our gifts to create wealth for Kingdom endeavors. I am surrounded by great prophets, but one of the greatest that I have ever seen is a person who has never prophesied in a church service. Bill Brehm is an incredibly gifted man of God in the area of finances. This man can prophesy about the fluid nature of the stock market. When the financial market crashed in 1998, we were still earning 25 percent in the stock market through the prophetic vision of this man.

Several years ago I was in a church where a young man prophesied in the service. Later, the pastor, the young man and I had lunch together. It was apparent that the pastor was excited about this young prophet and the great prophetic word he had given to the congregation that morning.

I said to the young man, "What do you do for a living, son?"

He replied, "Well, I'm a contractor."

"How're you doing financially?"

He said, "Not good, Brother Kelly."

"You know what your problem is?"

"What?"

"When it comes to your ministry gifts, you're an immature prophet."

The pastor almost fell out of his chair. The young man looked at me as if to say, "What are you talking about, Brother Kelly?"

I said, "This is what I'm talking about, son: When God gave the gifts of the Spirit in 1 Corinthians 12:1, the Scriptures say, 'Brothers, I do not want you to be ignorant.' And you're ignorant because you're only prophesying in church! When are you going to prophesy on where to get a business contract?"

I was in that church some time later and, after I spoke, they took an offering for me. The same young man came up afterwards and said, "I asked my pastor if I could give you my offering in private."

He handed me a very large check and said, "This is my offering to you, Brother Kelly. Since we last spoke my salary has gone from $26,000 to $126,000 in 12 months." He had begun to prophesy in the business realm and it helped his situation dramatically.

I believe in prosperity for the Christian (see Isa. 61:6). The problem is that most Christians just want to talk and claim prosperity but they won't put the hard labor into acquiring it. Part of that labor is using our gifts in the marketplace of the world to affect people. In turn, when the use of such gifts in the marketplace brings financial blessings, this harvest should be faithfully and consistently gathered into God's storehouses—local church efforts, citywide efforts by churches, and in worldwide mission endeavors.

DEPLOY THE TITHE WISELY FOR MAXIMUM SUCCESS

I was trained by the FBI as an intelligence officer in the Marine Corps and one of the first things they taught us was to follow the money. If you wanted to find out about a certain group or individual, find out where their money is going. If a pastor says that he tithes to his local church, missions or several different places, you would then know that he doesn't have a covering. The tithe must go to the covering, as in the case of the village, city and king's storehouses.

It's amazing how many churches don't tithe properly. They'll give for unusual reasons rather than from God's design. They'll give to a person they don't even like because they know a cousin or brother. Churches need to give to their mirror images – in other words, to those who reflect their vision in world missions, church planting, doctrine, church government, etc.

How many traveling ministers or TV evangelists have you seen that are money manipulators? They'll try to get as many people on their mailing list as they can so they can send their mailings to them to raise money. This blind raising of money leads to absurd abuses of believers. For instance, a friend of mine got three letters from a minister who sent prophetic words for my friend's father. The problem, however, was that my friend's father had died a year before. Money raised and applied in inappropriate ways hurts the Kingdom as deeply as no money raised at all.

Many genuine missionaries have to take just the crumbs off the table because local church leadership channels financial resources improperly. Many Christians are extremely under-funded. The local church needs to evaluate the worth of every traveling ministry and missionary and support the ones that are worthy. For some traveling ministries and missionaries it may be a scary move to see a church evaluating those they are funding, because the raising of standards would eliminate many from ministry. However, the standard needs to be raised. The church should want to see results and there has to be accountability. We can no longer send missionaries without accomplishing the things intended. We should not want to hear, "Well, I was in Africa for four years and led four people to Christ," or "I was in that foreign land but couldn't speak the language." We need to get all this silliness out of the ministry.

Acts 4:34&35 says, "From time to time those who owned land or houses sold them, brought the money from the sales and put it at the apostles' feet and it was distributed to anyone as he had need." The money that was placed at the apostles' feet wasn't for them to go and buy Jaguars or Mercedes Benzes but to provide for the needs in the Body. There are ministers today who take the money placed at their feet and buy big houses, big cars, fancy clothes and expensive jewelry. The majority of heathen millionaires live more simply than some of our top ministers. The money placed at the apostles' feet is to (1) give to the poor and (2) give to the prophets, evangelists, pastors, teachers, church plant-ers and missionaries.

I've had the opportunity to speak at conferences to ministers from various backgrounds. There is something I like to say to them about Church government. I say it for effect, hoping it will challenge ministers the way the Lord challenged me to look for the pattern of the Church. I say, "If someone who had a revolver pointed at your head said he would pull the trigger unless you gave him five Scriptures on Church government and how your church or ministry functions in it, how would you answer?" The vast majority of the ministers there would be shot because 90 percent don't have a clue about it. It is the only profession on earth where the men who lead the Church have no idea what Church government is. It's incredible!

We have seminaries and Bible Schools that teach on everything but the Church. You can go to school for two years and learn a great deal about the faith message, but not a thing about how the Church should be structured. These students are the ones who are being sent out to plant churches. How can we effectively plant a church when we know so little about its operation?

In the vision there is no serious challenge by the Army of God to the demonic forces in the valley. The reason: God's people are divided in efforts, ignorant of Church government as He designed it, and woefully deficient in understanding how the tithe helps the Church everywhere to overcome the enemy.

UNITY UNDER GOD'S BANNER

Then the Lord took me over the hill and into the next valley where I saw battalions so numerous I couldn't count them. The Lord said, "Each of these battalions represents men and women in my ministry."

Each battalion had a banner, and that banner was their identification. It was who they were; it was the banner they fought under. There was the discipleship banner, the faith banner, the deliverance banner, the holiness banner, the Calvinist banner, the charismatic banner, the shepherding banner, the Pentecostal banner and so forth. The battalions were groups and denominations in existence in the evangelical Church today.

Off in the distance I could see a very small battalion, but I could not see it clearly.

The Bible says that God has a banner over us (see Song of Sol. 2:4), but in this vision nobody had God's banner. Each group was under its own banner that identified who they were and how they were separate and distinct from other groups. Each group was full of pride, and each was confident that it would be the one who would win the war against the enemy.

As Christians, we must use the patterns for government and organization God gives the Church, we must give regularly and with discernment to various churches and ministries, and we must use our gifts to advance the Kingdom in the world. However, we must also encourage unity that allows for diversity of opinion and approach, and we must covenant to work together to fight the gates of hell.

UNITY OF DIVERSITY

Winning the war against the enemy will take a unity of diversity—a coming together in our uniqueness and differences. Can you imagine a football team where everybody is an offensive tackle? They could make a lot of noise and look really intimidating, but they couldn't throw, catch, kick or do a lot of other things. How about a basketball team with all seven-foot centers? They would have trouble dribbling the ball past half-court. It will take diversity in the Body of Christ to win in the same way it takes diversity for a football or basketball team to win.

God is not looking for a specific theology or any silly conformity; He's looking for a certain kind of individual—a person who wants to build according to His pattern. He wants people who are strong in character and integrity and who will build a ministry according to excellence – men and women whose yes is yes and no is no, individuals whose faces are like those of lions.

MAKING COVENANT IN WAR

When I was a Marine Corps officer, we were told by drill instructors and commanding officers that we would fight for the United States—not for ourselves, our units or our families—just the United States. But whether we were in training or in our best military dress, if it ever came to a *real* fight, a *real* war, we would certainly know better. The truth was we would fight for our lives and we would fight for our buddies in the platoon. Foxholes are where you'll find real covenant because people are fighting for their lives. If persecution ever breaks out in this land, Christians would covenant with one another overnight. We would forget all the silly conformity, the pet doctrines and the nonessential programs because we would be at war against a common enemy.

I've heard it taught that the greatest hindrance to covenant is that a person does not want a close relationship, but I think the greatest hindrance to making a covenant with another person is a lack of courage—we aren't secure in who we are in Christ.

Our security and identity in Christ are powerful. After all, how can I hurt you if I'm walking in Him? When you walk in me (my human will), you'll get hurt. When I walk in you (your human will), I'll get hurt. But when you walk in Him, you can't get hurt. God is looking for individuals who will walk in covenant like David and Jonathan. They weren't just two Jewish guys who liked one another; they were warriors who were in covenant (see 1 Sam. 14; 17—20; 23:15-18). Covenant is when true warriors come together for the purpose of warfare. Warfare goes beyond friendship. We are in covenant so that *collectively* we might slay the enemy; we are in covenant so that *collectively* we can go into the harvest field and set the captives free.

THE DIFFERENT POSITIONS
WORKING IN COVENANT

Warfare is the number-one role of the apostle. Prophets will woo you with the Word of the Lord. Teachers will educate you. Pastors will help you through your problems and hurts. Evangelists will get folks saved — but it is the apostle who will declare war on the enemy and lead the Church to war. The apostle is the one who will unify the Church into a fighting force. The apostle is the one who will bring all past and present truth and every past and present move of God to bear against the enemy.

If an apostle does not think and operate beyond his own generation—transgenerational—he is not an apostle. A sad indictment against the Church today is that there are fathers who will not allow their sons and daughters to go beyond them. When Jesus spoke to His disciples in John 14:12 He said that we will do greater works than He. We can do greater works than Jesus because He is in heaven and is totally behind us. Spiritual fathers should want to see their sons and daughters go beyond them in wisdom and success and do greater works for the sake of the Kingdom.

THE GOAL OF WARRIORS

One of the reasons the Church isn't reaching more Americans is because of bad theology. New believers get saved and say, "I just got saved and filled with the Holy Ghost, and I'm just waiting for Jesus to come." The Bible never says to sit around and idly wait until Jesus comes back. It does say to "look forward to the day of God and speed its coming" (2 Pet. 3:12), "to wait for his Son from heaven" (1 Thess. 1:10) and to eagerly want His coming (see Rev. 22:20).

What God actually said was, "occupy until I come" (Luke 19:13, *KJV*). That word "occupy" is a military and economic term. Militarily, it means to take possession of land that has been fought over and is now under martial law. Economically it means to keep making profit. What He meant was to be progressively making profit and progressively taking the earth until He returns.

When Jesus comes back, He'll be coming back for a Bride made up of a corporate expression—called the Church. He is not coming back for any kind of denomination or group, but a certain kind of Church. He is not coming back for the unbelieving Church or the make-believing Church. He's coming for the believing Church that is without spot or wrinkle (see Eph. 5:27).

In Gideon's day, God was looking for men who lapped water like dogs (see Judg. 7:4-7). There was the enemy, right there, and they looked at the enemy and licked up the water from their hands. They were thinking, *As soon as I get through drinking, I'm coming after you and you're all going to die.* Those who didn't lap like a dog were unprepared and God took them out of the front lines of the battle with the Midianites. Even today, there are Christians who lack vigilance and they are out of the front lines of the battle.

Vigilant warriors know how God organizes the Church, the role of regular giving to the Church, the use of gifts in the secular world, and the nature of unity in covenant. Vigilant warriors are always prepared to fight and their readiness brings ultimate victory.

CHAPTER FOUR

RIGID FORMATIONS FAIL

LEGALISM, ABUSIVE LEADERSHIP, FEAR AND LACK OF CORPORATE ANOINTING

The Warrior said to me, "Do you want to have some fun?"
"Yes," I said, perhaps a bit tentatively.
"Watch this."

The Warrior blew His trumpet and all the Lord's troops rose from their camps and marched into the field. They swarmed over the hill, heading toward the enemy camp, but before they reached the battle line, they all stopped.

Each battalion then formed a circle and began to walk in precision. One of the battalions was very precise. Another battalion was holding hands and dancing. Other battalions danced in various ways, turning and twisting to music only

they could hear. Other battalions just stood in their circles,
but all the battalions were in this formation.

I was a little surprised that the Warrior would ask me if I wanted to have some fun. I believe God does have a sense of humor and I'm convinced that we sometimes take ourselves too seriously. In the New Testament Jesus was most critical of the teachers of the law (see Matt. 23) who had reduced true worship to a stale formality and rote religious activity. The book of Jude was also extremely critical of false teachers who acted out of greed and selfish ambition. These two groups took themselves too seriously; they never entered the joy of the Lord. They were always protecting their false image and trying to win the respect of others with their false piety.

LOOSEN UP

Christians need to loosen up at times, let our hair down and become real. That's why on the last night of our 1996 Men in Ministry Conference, I decided to do something to loosen things up. As the head apostle of Antioch Churches and Ministries, I was scheduled to speak on the final night (something I had done for a number of years). This night, when I came into the conference hall, I was wearing an outrageously bright blue suit. I bought the suit in Detroit, Michigan, at a bargain outlet. It was really cheap and I thought it would be great fun to wear on some special occasion. When I entered the hall that night there were some comments and snickers, but it wasn't until I got to the pulpit to bring my message that one, then two, then a whole bunch of the guys started to snicker. So I said, "Well, men, when you're old and ugly, you gotta try harder." Then everybody started to roar. It was a great laugh for all of us. I didn't mind their laughing; in fact, I think things like that help our relationships.

I want all Christians to be unencumbered from any distortions that prompt us to be over-religious and phony. We shouldn't have to put on a facade when we're in fellowship. We are real people—flawed and ordinary—but with an outward vision and dynamic purpose of mind to build the Kingdom.

IN THE BATHROOM

People relate better when they're having fun. We shouldn't get offended when our friends poke a little fun at us. I wonder how many times the story has been told about senior pastor Ed Mannering of Restoration Family Church in North Richland Hills, Texas, who had to go to the bathroom in the middle of a Sunday service. He still had on his lapel microphone when he was standing at the urinal and said, "I hope we have a good offering today." All the church heard him.

Ed laughs along with whoever tells that story about him. He's secure in who he is in Christ and who he is as a man. He is secure in the ministry God has given him. He has planted churches in New Jersey, Michigan and Texas and has raised up many leaders who are now in fivefold ministry, full time. He has been an incredible blessing to many people because he is free to be himself.

YOU IMPART WHAT YOU ARE

Senior pastor Dion Boffo of Samaritan Fellowship in Bibbsboro, New Jersey, pointed out, "No matter what a leader teaches, people will become what the leader is. You impart what you are and not what you talk about, such as kids who always catch more than is taught. You can teach and teach and teach, but did you ever watch kids? They pick their nose the same way their mom or dad does. They cough, they sit, they have mannerisms, they scratch the way dad does. Kids pick up all kinds of things. You ask, 'Where did they learn that?' Your wife says, 'They learned it from you! You scratch like that.'"

In the vision, the funny thing about the battalions was not that they reacted to the trumpet, but *how* they reacted to the trumpet. They reacted like Pavlov's dogs that automatically salivated at the sound of a bell. In the same fashion, the battalions heard the trumpet and they gave a conditioned response. It was a formality – a formula they had learned from the group to which they belonged. These responses proved worthless against the enemy.

THE BATTALION DANCED, TWISTED AND FORMED CIRCLES

When the battalions heard the trumpet, they did what they were taught to do—the only thing they knew how to do. Some danced, twisted and formed circles, and did it all with great precision, but they never got to the enemy camp. What they had learned, they learned well, because they did it with precision; obviously they had put a lot of hard work into what they had learned.

The only way to properly discern the sound of the trumpet is with the corporate anointing. The battalions weren't hearing well and their ministries (dancing, twisting, forming circles, etc.), which they were carrying out with precision, were totally ineffective.

There is nothing worse than a young person looking for a model for his ministerial career and being caught up in an old paradigm. If our young ministers follow the old road of professional ministry and conform to the status quo, they will one day end up in the same circle, doing the same silly things. What the Kingdom needs is Kingdom builders.

DANGERS WE FACE

The Church faces obstacles that can destroy our effectiveness against the enemy just as the battalions were rendered powerless.

These obstacles include: *legalism* which has a form of godliness but denies the power and joy in Christ; *autocratic leaders* who misuse godly zeal and wound other believers; *wrong priorities* in building the Kingdom; and *fear* that prevents others from excelling in Christ.

LEGALISM

A friend of mine was saved in a very legalistic Pentecostal church. Everything in that church was called sin—except breathing. Going to movies was sinful, wearing certain kinds of clothing was sinful and long hair on a man was sinful. As a child he went to see the movie *Mary Poppins,* and it took him six months to get over the feelings of guilt. When he was older and was called to preach, he preached and acted in the same fashion he had been raised in. Inside the place of worship he never told any jokes, and outside the church sanctuary he was never lighthearted or frivolous because for him such things were nothing less than sin. What a powerless and joyless way to live in Christ!

God wants to send forth an army with His anointing that will smash the strongholds of hell, enter strong-walled cities and shatter the power of the enemy. Sad to say, God's Army, the Church, is often crippled by legalism. This attitude makes it hard for people to be genuine with one another.

In Christ's day the religious, legalistic phonies were a type and shadow of the Dark Ages to come. When Emperor Constantine declared Christianity to be the religion of the state, the Church began to lose its genuine power and joy. The moment the Church stopped being an enemy of the world, it became a submitted friend of the world. The Church gradually lost all its power, and its priesthood became not all that different from the priesthood of the Greco-Roman Empire. Even the secular historians call it the "Dark Ages" which means "the light is not among us." The

Church was a political entity—powerless, joyless, only a shell.

AUTOCRATIC LEADERS

Bruce Gunkle, who pastors City of Refuge Christian Fellowship in San Antonio, Texas, tells a story of his experience in the Air Force that sounds very similar to the training that the battalions in the vision had received. Bruce was in the military (before he was saved) for 21 years and was a colonel for part of that time. At one point he had command of several hundred people who guarded B-52s and a storage area in Minot, North Dakota. In the winter, Minot can dip to 80° below zero. When it's that cold the townspeople bring in their dogs from outside. But the B-52s and the storage area still had to be guarded, so the young guards had to stay out and do their job in the chilling air. Yhey were treated worse than dogs. Trust me — 18-year-old military guards don't want to walk around carrying guns in that kind of weather.

In the previous 21 months, the Army had seven different people in charge, all of whom got fired because they couldn't handle demands of the post. At the time Bruce had the reputation of a leader who could get things done and make things happen. Bruce was in charge of that facility for nearly two years and the outfit did very well under his watch. His philosophy was, "The new broom sweeps clean." When he took over, he really took over. His commanding presence sent a message to those 18- to 20-year-old guards. They feared Bruce more than going out in 80-below weather because they knew if they messed up and crossed the line, Bruce would make them pay a price.

Bruce's style at that time was very autocratic. In the military, such command may have some merit, but a similar style in the Church is not effective. You may say, "Well, the Air Force is like that, but that could never happen in a church." But it does happen all the time in churches, only these autocratic spiritual lead-

RIGID FORMATIONS FAIL   63

ers will do things slightly different, in a subtler way that is not healthy or productive for the Kingdom.

Over the years I predicted the fall of three apostolic networks. I didn't want to see the fall of these networks, but it happened. It happened because of improper use of spiritual authority and principles. These groups were provoking their sons to wrath by heavy-handed leadership. It wasn't a matter of if they would fail. It was just a matter of when.

A heavy-handed or manipulative style brings enormous casualties and wounds among believers. People become inhibited and will shun certain positive functions in a church environment because of past hurts born from autocratic abuses.

HEALING A PAST WOUND

Joe Warner, pastor of Freedom Fellowship Church in Orlando, Florida, tells his story of spiritual abuse and his subsequent healing. It began one Sunday morning as he was preaching:

> As I began to preach, I saw a cloud come into the room and begin to form itself into a shape that looked just like a hand. The hand came and rested over the top of me, and the Lord began to speak to me as I was trying to preach. I was looking around, hoping someone else would see this, but no one else did. The Lord spoke from the cloud and said, "It was apostolic ministry that wounded you, so it will take apostolic ministry to heal you."
>
> "What does the cloud represent, Lord?"
>
> The Lord replied, "The cloud represents the fivefold ministry and a cover; that's what a cloud does. If you seek proper biblical government and authority to come under, there will be a level of healing that you need. Not only that, but it will rain [there will be a blessing]."

That (apostolic ministry) was a really big issue
with me because I was part of a network that literally
destroyed men. I really began to wrestle with God. I didn't
want anything to do with anything apostolic; it made me
want to throw up. I wanted nothing to do with that type
of thing, but I knew it was biblical. If you go to Ephesians
4, you can't get away from apostolic ministry, can you?
The Church is founded on an apostolic and prophetic
foundation. We can't escape that. Finally after two or
three weeks of wrestling with God I said, "All right, if
there is a relational network out there, one that won't
come in and be a dictator in my life, then I am willing
to consider it." That was as far as I was willing to go at
the time. The next day I met Gary Gonzalez (a missionary to Spanish-speaking countries) and another brother.
This other brother had the same story I had. He sat there
at lunch and told me my story without me opening my
mouth. I was convinced that it was the sovereignty of
God!

So I began to go through the process of checking
out Antioch Churches and Ministries (ACM). I really
put them through the mill! I wanted to know everything; I wanted to know how every dime was spent;
I wanted to know how the authority structure worked;
I wanted to know what qualified someone to be an
apostle; on and on and on. I had thousands of questions. I had been part of another network; I helped plan
conferences for that network. I knew all the big shots in
that network; I knew what really went on. I knew the
right questions to ask. So I went through the process
of becoming a part of ACM. John Kelly would show up
and spend time with me, and while that may not sound

like a big deal to you, it is when you're used to guys who would come into town and only relate to the senior pastor and no one else. For the head apostle to come in and want to spend time with me and the men in my church was an unusual surprise.

I said, "What do you want to do Kelly; do you want to sit around a boardroom table?"

"No! Let's go to the mall," Kelly told me.

He wanted to go to the mall; he wanted to hang out with me. He wanted to find out who I was. I wasn't used to that kind of thing. I was used to sitting around in three-piece suits and having major conversations. I was used to being talked down to instead of someone relating to me. This was like another world; I didn't know quite what to do with it. So we went to the mall and had our discussions there.

MINISTRIES THAT HAVE LEADERS WHO ARE OBSESSED WITH BUILDING THEIR OWN HOUSE (THEIR MINISTRY) OVER BUILDING THE HOUSE OF GOD HAVE THEIR PRIORITIES ALL WRONG.

WRONG PRIORITIES

Joe Warner's positive experience with ACM contrasts sharply with some ministries where leaders have used their authority to abuse others, but this isn't the only problem God's people face. Some ministries have leaders who are obsessed with building their own house (their ministry) over building the house of God (see Ps. 127:1; Hag. 1:8,9). Their priorities are all wrong.

Joe points out that the group where he had been wounded had a number of men who were qualified to plant churches. They could preach, teach and they were anointed—they could do it all. Nevertheless they were held down—suppressed—because the leadership's attitude was "build my house." There was no mind-set of releasing; there was no mind-set of wanting their sons to exceed them. The leadership wanted their sons to stay and build their house. How sad. The true function of the present-day apostolic reformation is to build the house of God in preparation for the second coming of Christ.

THE FEAR AMONG THE MEN OF EPHRAIM

Psalm 78:9 says, "The men of Ephraim, though armed with bows, turned back on the day of battle." The Ephraimites looked ready and acted ready, but when it came time to go to war, they turned back. Why? They were unprepared to really go into battle. They could claim it and make bold proclamations, but they were not prepared for battle. Their fathers before them had not prepared them. They had forgotten God and had become fearful. Fear causes believers to do many foolish things in the name of Christ.

The troops in my vision had formed circles and were very precise in what they were doing. They thought they had it all, but they were steeped in legalism, formality and rigidity—so much so that the Warrior thought it was funny. Not funny in a cute way, but funny because it was preposterous that the Body of Christ could behave in that manner when we have the Word of God to direct us. What the Warrior was showing me was the poor preparation among the sons and daughters of God for the day of battle. What the Army of God was missing is critical for victory—corporate anointing.

NO CORPORATE ANOINTING

Meanwhile the enemy soldiers had come out of their camp and were waiting for God's Army to engage them in battle. When the Army of God formed their circles, showing no signs of engaging the enemy, the little enemy warriors went to the battalions of the Army of God and began to pelt them with small daggers, arrows, sticks and stones. The demons cursed and laughed at them, mocking the Lord's Army. Three enemy platoons surrounded the circles that the Army of God had formed.

From the midst of the fray, I could hear the soldiers of God screaming, "We're at war! We're at war! This is war! We are the Army of God!"

At first it was thrilling to see the Army of God on the battlefield with their corporate anointing. Then the Warrior brought me closer and I could see the enemy mocking them.

Then the Army of God turned around and went back to the valley they had come from.

The Army of God was screaming, "We're at war! This is war!" Men who have been in the war with Iraq (Desert Storm) say this is a natural reaction. Even with the months of preparation, when Desert Storm actually began, the reaction was "We're at war! This is war!" The realization would suddenly hit them that they were in a real life-and-death conflict! Fear, unbelief, panic and all kinds of emotions suddenly rise to the surface under such pressures.

In the vision the Army of God was screaming, "We're at war!

This is war!" But there was no real war. They were merely being pelted by little demons.

LIMITED BOUNDARIES OF RELEVANT FELLOWSHIP

I wondered how the enemy could attack the Army of God and why the Army of God would not retaliate. Then I knew! There was no corporate anointing. At first I thought there was, but there wasn't. The Army of God would not leave their own circles and allow their anointing to flow with those in the other circles. Those circles were their limited boundaries of relevant fellowship and vision. The soldiers in the circles were so inwardly focused, they had no idea what was going on around them. They could not discern the voice of God (the trumpet) and they didn't attack the enemy because there was no corporate anointing.

MAY THEY BE BROUGHT TO COMPLETE UNITY

In John 17:23, Jesus prayed, "May they be brought to complete unity to let the world know that you sent me." There are two things in this passage that Jesus prayed for that have not yet happened in Christian history. He prayed for unity and He prayed that the world would know He was sent by the Father. When the Body of Christ does come into unity, the world will know. The Body will come into unity, and when it does the world will be astounded because it has never seen true unity. Some sports teams and organizations may have some surface unity, but the world has never seen real covenantal unity on a large scale.

SELF-APPOINTED

Instead of staying in our circles thinking we have it all, we have to reach out in true fellowship. Sometimes we think we have it all, but it's obvious to everyone around us that we don't.

Once I was in Mexico City with apostle Gary Gonzalez. He and I had an opportunity to listen to a self-appointed apostle from the United States who happened to be there. He walked out on the stage and said, "I'm apostle so-and-so from Oklahoma," and he began to preach, saying, "Praise the Lord, Hallelujah, praise the Lord, glory, thanks be to God." He was saying these things in his best baritone, Pentecostal voice.

The translator said to the audience, "All he's doing is hollering out clichés. When he starts saying something worthwhile I'll let you know; meanwhile I'll give the announcements." Eventually the poor translator ran out of announcements, so he got his notes out of his Bible and preached his own sermon. The translator preached a much better message than the self-appointed apostle who continued to yell out clichés.

INCREASE THE ANOINTING

It is not difficult to experience a greater anointing on ministry and break out of the circles of formality and legalism that are a hindrance to the Kingdom. Apostle Gary Kivelowitz, an apostolic administrator with ACM, is a great example of a man increasing the anointing on his ministry. About nine years ago, Gary was pastoring The Church of the Messiah in New Jersey. He called me and said, "How do I get the church really rolling in the Holy Ghost and growing with evangelism and all that stuff?"

The person who came instantly to mind was Jimmy Mas, pastor of Covenant Life Christian Church in Sunrise, Florida. I encouraged Gary, "You need to get in touch with Pastor Jimmy Mas and have him come and impart to you and your church the anointing for the helps ministry and training leaders."

Gary replied, "But John, I know how to do that."

"Oh."

"John, what else?"

I went through four things that I thought he should do.

"But John, I know how to do that."

I replied, "Oh."

Gary persisted, "So, John, how can you help me?"

"Brother, I can't help you. According to you, it's all flowing right."

Gary finally got the point. He had Jimmy Mas come and impart his anointing for raising up leaders. That was nine years ago and that anointing is still flowing today.

A few years later, Gary's church, Church of the Messiah, was dry. During this dry time he heard that senior pastor Tony Germano's congregation, Victorious Life Christian Church in upstate New York, was having a wave of revival. He met with his elders and told them, "We don't need a deposit of that. I don't want it to come and visit us for the weekend, leaving us to remember it and talk about it for the next year. I want it flowing in our church. I want that anointing to be exponentially flowing in our church." So he called Tony, with whom he was very good friends.

Gary said, "Tony, I hear you're having revival in your church— I need it!"

"What would you like me to do?" Tony asked.

"Tony, you're the doctor; you write the prescription. You have the anointing; you tell me!" Gary continued to explain that he didn't just want a deposit; he wanted the anointing to flow for years to come. "Tony, you tell me how I can get this anointing to flow in our church."

"Gary, the first thing you need to do is get all of your leaders who can get time off work, and get in a couple of vans and drive up to our meetings and sit under it for a few nights." Tony replied.

Gary did that! You know why? He wanted to flow in that anointing. A bunch of his leaders spent a couple of days at Tony's services.

Then Tony said, "Take it back, and in a month or two I'll come down and visit you. After I come to visit, we'll keep in touch."

They did that and after a couple of months, they received the refreshing at their church. That refreshing is still flowing, long after Gary left that church as its pastor.

Then there was a time that Gary's home groups were dead. Gary did all that he knew to do. He even prophesied to the dead, but the dead remained dead. Finally God spoke to him and asked him this question: "Who do you know that has a very strong anointing in bringing life to home meetings?"

Gary answered, "Well, Lord, pastor John Diana of Pittsburgh Word and Worship!"

Gary made a phone call to John and shared with him how he had a problem with home meetings (cell groups) and how he needed some life in them.

Gary said, "John, I'm not looking for a good idea. I need a flow of an anointing that is going to go for years and years and be mixed with my anointing and the anointing of this church. I don't want just a good idea or something to pump us up for a weekend. Can you help us?"

John asked, "What do you want me to do?"

"You're the doctor!"

"Well, you know what I suggest? I suggest that I send Rick and Natalie Paladin to you. If you'll receive them, I believe God will use them for an ongoing flow in your ministry." (Rick was the copastor at Greater Pittsburgh Word and Worship.)

Gary wasn't offended. Although he was calling for the head person, there was someone else whom the head person recommended. Gary had Rick and Natalie Paladin come in, and after they spent some time there, Gary stayed in contact by phone for a couple of months being coached by them. Life was brought to the home groups and that life was still flowing many years later.

A HEAD ON A HORSE

Gary recalled the time at the first Men in Ministry Conference he attended when a prophet stood and prophesied. He prophesied in a very strong and loud voice and said, "Jesus is riding in the room on a white horse. The problem is that the only thing on the horse is a head. There is no body; everyone wants to receive from the head only. However, Jesus calls us to receive from the rest of the Body. We need those other anointings flowing in our ministry. If we would just humble ourselves and break out of our little circles and ask, then we would receive."

JEHU—A TYPE OF APOSTLE

Jehu was an Old Testament figure who broke out of his circle and was resolute in carrying out the task God had commanded him to do. In 2 Kings 9, Elisha sends a young prophet to anoint Jehu as king over Israel. The young prophet finds Jehu sitting around with some other army officers and calls him into an inner room where he makes the proclamation Elisha sent him to deliver.

When he comes out of the inner room, the other officers ask him, "Why did this madman come to you?" (2 Kings 9:11).

Jehu responds by saying, "You know the man and the sort of things he says" (v. 11). In other words, you know how those prophets are—they're a little goofy.

When Jehu tells his fellow officers that the young prophet had anointed him king over Israel, they spread their cloaks for him and shout, "Jehu is King!" (v. 13).

Immediately, Jehu and his men set out for Jezreel. As they approached Jezreel, King Joram of Israel sends out horsemen to see if Jehu is coming in peace. The horsemen ask, "Do you come in peace?" (vv. 18,19).

Jehu responds, "What do you have to do with peace? Fall in behind me" (v. 19). In other words, don't get in my way or else you will die.

When King Joram of Israel approached Jehu by chariot, Jehu put an arrow between Joram's shoulders, killing him.

When Jezebel heard what had happened, she "painted her eyes, arranged her hair and looked out of a window" (v. 30). Jehu, without hesitation, called out, "Who is on my side?" (v. 32).

Some eunuchs, who were standing nearby, responded to him. Jehu said, "Throw her down" (v. 33). They did it, and that was the end of Jezebel.

Jehu then killed the 70 sons of the house of Ahab, all the relatives, and all the priests of Baal. Jehu didn't fiddle-faddle around trying to orchestrate a formula; he simply gathered his men and went about carrying out the will of the Lord.

Jehu is a type and shadow of the apostle. The apostle will gather his men who want to go to spiritual war against Satan's demonic forces and engage them wherever they may be found. God's Army will not be pelted by sticks and stones of the enemy, nor will they allow the enemy to mock them as the Army of God did in my vision.

MEN OF VALOR

The apostolic army will gather men of valor from various backgrounds who are unified, and aggressively pursue the forces of the enemy. That is the way a network is supposed to work. It's a give-and-take ministry where everyone benefits. The reason the enemy platoons were able to attack the Army of God was because they were in their own little circles separated from the rest of the Body instead of being unified. They were isolated and alone, trying to wage a war that they were incapable of fighting alone (see Eccles. 4:9-12).

CHAPTER FIVE

WASTING THE TROOPS

WHEN POOR LEADERSHIP SQUANDERS GOD'S CHILDREN

What I saw next horrified me. I said, "No, this vision is not of God. I rebuke it in the name of Jesus!" The vision then stopped. This happened one night as I was in prayer.

On another night I had the same dream. I was in the same place as in the first dream and I saw the same vile happenings. Again I said, "I rebuke this in the name of Jesus. This dream is not of God."

Repeatedly the Warrior said to me, "You will speak this at Men in Ministry." He wanted me to share this vision at our upcoming men's conference.

I was later given the same dream and vision, but as I

was about to rebuke it, a voice said to me, "If you rebuke Me,
the Lord your God, one more time, I will rebuke you! You
will speak of this vision!"

I was appalled at what I saw then! The men from the
battalions had formed circles and they were spilling their seed
on the ground.

I said, "God, what is this foul, lustful, sexual thing I am
seeing?"

God said, "It is none of that. Get your mind out of that
place; that's not what I am talking about. What you see are
men and women in ministry wasting the seed of My anoint-
ing by not producing spiritual sons and daughters. Yes, they
preach, prophesy and exercise spiritual gifts over My people,
but they are not building into My people. They are waste-
ful! Doesn't the Word speak of My incorruptible seed and
the corruptible seed? What I am showing you is that My
incorruptible seed can be corrupted by the wasteful use and
dissipation of My anointing."

That was the scene I kept seeing; it was particularly horrify-
ing. That is why I kept rebuking it until the Lord threatened to
rebuke me. My first thought was, *How is the anointing wasted?*
The Army of God was wasting the anointing by spilling their
seed on the ground. As I thought about this, it became apparent.
The anointing is wasted and our seed is spilled on the ground
when we don't build according to the biblical pattern and pass on
a spiritual legacy.

The men were casting their seed inward, toward their own
inward vision. Their sin was not a sexual sin, but a sin against the
image of God. They were not producing disciples for the next
generation; they were using men to carry out their own personal
vision, not the larger vision of Kingdom building.

All Christians are given a personal vision, but along with a personal vision we are given a vision for our marriage, our church, our city, etc. We must let the personal vision serve the larger vision. The personal vision must submit to the marriage vision; the marriage vision must submit to the church vision; the church vision must submit to the city vision, etc. In letting the personal vision die in order to serve the larger vision (marriage, church, city, etc.), God will then resurrect our personal vision and allow us to walk in it. These men were serving their own personal vision with no regard for the larger vision.

THE SIN OF ONAN

In Genesis 38:8-10, Onan was told to lie with his brother's wife so he might produce offspring for his dead brother.

> Then Judah said to Onan, "Lie with your brother's wife and fulfill your duty to her as a brother-in-law to produce offspring for your brother." But Onan knew that the offspring would not be his; so whenever he lay with his brother's wife, he spilled his semen on the ground to keep from producing offspring for his brother. What he did was wicked in the Lord's sight; so he put him to death also.

Onan was serving his own personal vision. Since the offspring would not be his, he spilled his seed on the ground. The Church has many Onans today who see only their own personal vision. God has given them His vision for their church and city, but they have no regard for the propagation of the gospel beyond their own lifetime. If they don't own it or can't control it, they (like Onan) don't want it. Consequently, like Onan, they will do the wickedness of spilling their seed.

A bona fide, God-given vision can sometimes lead to much error if the person receiving the vision uses every and any means to see that vision fulfilled. There is only one way to fulfill any God-given vision and that is to build the Kingdom. There is only one way to build the Kingdom and that is to build the Kingdom into people. The most grievous error is to use people to fulfill a vision without building the Kingdom into them and releasing them into their calling.

If a church leader spills his seed in the circle by building his own agenda and not pollinating the seed, God will not allow that leader to self-pollinate. Consequently, there will be no successful ministry to the next generation.

A DIME A DOZEN

All Christians are anointed, but if we face inward and spill our seed, the anointing is wasted. Pastor Jimmy Mas says, "[Anointed leaders] are a dime a dozen; there are a lot of anointed leaders." This is true; the leaders of some of the largest churches in this country are outrageously soulish—they manipulate the gifting of others to build their own ministry and cause believers to prostitute themselves for the sake of the leader's vision.

We have this glut of anointed, soulish leaders today because their predecessors had the same mind-set and developed them. Each new generation of soulish leaders takes their place in the circle, replacing the former soulish leaders, and they continue to cast their seed inward.

My personal opinion is that no megachurch has ever gone into the second generation successfully. If you were to take a survey of the history of megachurches in America, I believe you would find the vast majority of these buildings sitting empty or occupied by only a handful of people. These large empty edifices are the result of men not building according to the biblical pattern but instead using the giftings of others to build their personal kingdoms. Megachurches are large for a reason. They refuse to release their sons to be sent out and/or to plant a church. They keep them in their house so they can continue to serve the leader's vision.

Mas contrasts this self-centered leadership with those nurtured in biblical principles. "When you train your people or your leaders to live by biblical principles, they will still live by what they've been taught even when things get flowery or disastrous. In fact, they'll have little regard for those who don't live by them."

THE ANTIOCH VERSUS THE
JERUSALEM CHURCH MODEL

The New Testament Church at Antioch is the pattern for the modern church. It was a church that sent out missionaries and evangelists and planted churches (see Acts 13:1-4). To send and plant should be the goal of every church because this is the pattern in the Scriptures.

Jerusalem is the model for apostolic ministry. However, it is a poor model for church planting and for local church development. In the Jerusalem model we see a megachurch where thousands were saved and the presence of the local leadership kept other believers in the city (see Acts 2—6). This hindered effective expansion of the kingdom (until persecution forced the leadership to plant other churches abroad). Clearly, megachurches that do not actively send out missionaries and plant new churches will not survive the second generation.

There is nothing wrong with building a large church; I don't mean to imply that at all. If a pastor is building according to the pattern by sending and planting, God will certainly bless that work. However, for Kingdom expansion, it is better to have 10 churches of 100 people, than to have 1 church of 1,000 people. It's been proven that the most effective method of evangelism is to plant churches.

But megachurches are often deficient in helping their people develop their ministries. Oddly, many people will go to a megachurch for exactly that reason—they want to learn and have an opportunity to minister. What they discover is just the opposite. The large church and the small church have virtually the same demands and number of opportunities to serve in ministry. The only difference between the two congregations is that the opportunity to serve and grow in ministry is greater in a smaller church.

Think about it. How many elders does a church of 1,000 need? Maybe six. How many elders does a church of 150 need? Probably six. How many preachers does a church of 1,000 need on a Sunday morning? One. How many preachers does a church of 150 need on a Sunday morning? One. How about Sunday School, teen ministry, deacons, ushers, teachers, etc.?

There is obviously much more opportunity in a small church than in a megachurch. It is obvious why 10 churches of 100 members are more effective in finding the lost than one church of 1,000. There are so many more people integrated into the ministry.

LEADERSHIP DEVELOPMENT

The fivefold ministry is supposed to "prepare God's people for works of service, so that the Body of Christ may be built up" (Eph. 4:12). The leadership should prepare the people of God for works of service to build up the kingdom of God. It isn't for the building up of our ministry or vision, it's for the building of the kingdom of God. This can only be done with a releasing mentality so that those prepared for ministry can be sent and/or can go plant.

Larry Kreider, an apostolic overseer of Dove Christian

International in Ephrata, Pennsylvania, who pastored a church of more than 2,000, says he went through some shifting and sorting before the Lord called him to an apostolic movement. So at the end of January 1996, they split the large church into many smaller ones. They had viable, functioning cell groups, so they had the leadership already in place through their leadership development. The key for them came 15 years ago when the Lord put it on their hearts to train spiritual fathers in small groups and to train leaders for the work of the ministry. Otherwise it would have been an impossible task. Now they have hundreds of people taking on new roles as leaders and elders. Through this they are not just maintaining spiritual children, but raising up spiritual fathers.

UP THE CHURCH LADDER

Pastor Ray Guinn of Family Life Christian Center in Houston, Texas, tells of his experience being with a denomination. He says that when he went to pastor a church, he knew he wasn't going to be there very long. The Babylonian churches (as he calls them) he had been in had a paradigm like this: You were in a profession and on a corporate ladder. If you wanted to be successful in ministry, you had to ultimately go up the ladder. What many would do is get the monthly newsletter to see what opportunities had opened up at larger churches and in the secrecy of their bedrooms or studies, they would get their resumé and apply for the opening. This is what's out there in Christendom and what has taken place in many settings. Pastor Guinn goes on to say:

> Back in the '70s, we had a lot of teaching centers that were springing up all over the country. However, there is more to ministry than seeing people as someone to teach so we might get fulfillment from teaching. There

A TRUE

SPIRITUAL FATHER

WOULD

WANT TO

SEE HIS SON FULLY

DEVELOPED,

MATURED

AND

GROUNDED,

STRONG,

STEADFAST

AND

SUCCESSFUL IN

THE THINGS

OF GOD.

are many instructors—people who want to gather people to themselves. They love to have a crowd, because they love the thrill and joy of teaching (being in the pulpit).

Nevertheless, God hasn't called us to develop teaching centers. He has called spiritual fathers who would also take the responsibility to be a father. There are a lot of people who are birthing, but who don't want to raise spiritual children. They want to birth them, then say, "I've had the pleasure of birthing these kids; now you take them and raise them! You nurture them! You love them! You admonish them! You be responsible for them." The result is, we're raising a generation of bastard children without fathers. The Holy Spirit has got to bring the Church to accountability; it has to bring the Church to understand that there is more to this than birthing.

A true spiritual father would want to see his son fully developed, matured and grounded, strong, steadfast and successful in the things of God. A true spiritual father would want to see his sons cut loose (sent out and/or planting) on their own and being successful. No true father would want to keep his son around the house so he could have him there to cut the grass and do the chores. Yet this is what is happening in the majority of our churches in America. The sons who are qualified to minister are kept at home when they should be cut loose to build the Kingdom.

THEIR OWN ELITIST BANNERS

The men in the circle were corrupting the incorruptible seed by wasteful use of the anointing. Some of them were professional fivefold ministers; others were lay ministers. They were so focused on their own vision, that they couldn't discern the trumpet call. They didn't know where the battle line was; they were ineffective at waging war; there was no corporate anointing, and they were under their own elitist banner. All the while they thought they were accomplishing something. They had an inward vision; they had taken a vision that God had given them and turned it inward, corrupting the anointing, because they had a perverse plan for Kingdom building.

There is one psalm that serves as an excellent picture of the Church today:

> Turn your steps toward these everlasting ruins, all this destruction the enemy has brought on the sanctuary. Your foes roared in the place where you met with us; they set up their standards as signs (Ps. 74:3,4).

The enemy has ravaged much of the Church – not by coming against it with full armies, but subtly, little by little. The enemy entered the sanctuary and did damage to everything that we call

Church; he has pulled down God's standards and raised up his own standards.

The men in the circle were cheering about how far certain individuals could cast their seed. Not only did they waste the anointing, but they even bragged about wasting it. This is perhaps the most arrogant, soulish thing someone could do—waste the anointing, then brag about it. Some of the men in the circle were proud of their own accomplishments—so proud in fact, that they were in competition with other men in seeing who could cast their seed the farthest. They didn't realize that if they just turned around and faced outward, it could have gone a lot farther. By turning around they would have had an outward vision for Kingdom building and could have used the anointing effectively.

The men in the circle who were casting their seed and competing with one another had no understanding of their calling. They were using their calling as a license to exalt themselves. The line between spiritual and secular was blurred because the secular was in everything they did.

There is no such blurring of spiritual and secular with pastor Luther Laite of Christian Life Family Church in Palm Bay, Florida. Luther has a maintenance business on the side and has a contract with several businesses in the Palm Bay area. One of the businesses is a Chevrolet dealer that is one of the top dealerships in the country. It's a real spit-and-polish, top-notch operation.

Luther's influence goes beyond making sure the place looks good. Through ministering the Word to the owner of the automobile business, Luther made him realize that he had some people working for him who weren't pleasing God. They were not honoring their marriage covenants.

As Laite ministered to the owner, the gentleman began to realize that God was withholding His blessing on his dealership because he was tolerating sin by not confronting some of his top producers. He had a meeting with them and said that he was going to put God first. In the process, noticing the owner's new sense of morality, especially on issues involving faithfulness to one's wife, the top producer left. The owner also made the decision to close the dealership on Sundays. This surprised his salespeople because Sunday was the biggest shopping day of the week. However, God blessed this fellow's desire to be an ethical and honorable owner. God has allowed his business to sell more cars on Saturday and Monday than he ever sold when he was open on Sunday.

Laite was God's instrument in creating Kingdom influence by sharing a standard that the owner embraced. The effect on the owner in turn brought about constructive change in the dealership.

The Line Between Secular and Spiritual

Keith Tucci, a church mobilizer from Pittsburgh, Pennsylvania, said this about the ministry:

> We need to annihilate the line between secular and spiritual, if we're going to be Kingdom people, if we're going to be the young lions—the young men who go out and take the Kingdom; the young men who are going to be the judges; the young men who are going to be the senators; the young men who are going to be doctors, bankers and entrepreneurs. The young men who are going to do these things have got to believe that they are there representing God.
>
> If you're a man of God, no matter what you do, you don't have a secular job. You may have some secular organization paying your missionary salary—that's OK. It's

not like from nine to five you belong to the world, then after that you belong to God. This type of thinking has put us in a position where the Church is in a defensive posture, instead of a offensive posture.

Paul and I truly believe that this viewpoint should be taken by everyone in ministry.

If someone is a Christian banker, he should have a vision of serving God as a Christian banker. Being a Christian and building the Kingdom don't begin after banking hours. The same thing goes for every profession, for serving God cannot be separated from what we do. Keith, who is a leader in the Right-to-Life movement, said:

> In my experience in dealing with authorities, the most dangerous people I've met have been professing Christians who are confused about who they are serving. The hardest punishment meted out to people who are doing righteous things, comes often from professing Christians.

Keith had a professing-Christian judge say to him, "Well, when I put this robe on, I belong to the state."
So Keith said, "I hope you don't die in that robe."

I'M PRO-LIFE, EXCEPT FOR...

On another occasion, a politician running for office went to visit Keith. This fellow was an outspoken, professing Christian and he wanted Keith to help in his campaign. Keith questioned him on what he believed and the subject turned to protecting the unborn.

The politician said, "Well, I'm pro-life except for..." and then started giving Keith the exceptions. By the time he was finished, it was obvious that he wasn't pro-life at all.

Keith said to him, "If you're going to run as a Christian, you don't have the authority to make those exceptions. No one has given you that liberty; no one has given that license."

The politician countered by telling Keith that it was fine for Keith to be a staunch pro-lifer, because he was a preacher.

This politician was raised in the Church and confessed Christ, but his reaction epitomize

sd a problem we have in the Church today. This man had no understanding of his calling. His purpose for running for office was because he was frustrated about some things that were happening. However the real reason for any believer to run for office is to advance the Kingdom and fulfill a calling. To make more money or have a better life isn't bad; it's just secondary to God's wanting each of us to be Kingdom builders.

ABUSED IN THE NAME OF CHRIST

There are many examples of people who have been abused in the name of Jesus—abused by "men" who would stand in the circle and face inward. Keith tells a story about a carpet cleaner who came to clean Keith's carpets a few years ago. He was an older gentlemen who was a church member. When the carpets were clean, Keith, pulling out his wallet, asked him how much he owed him.

The old gentleman said, "What do you mean?"

Keith said, "Well, how much does it cost?"

"You're going to pay me?"

"Well, of course."

"I just assumed since you were a preacher you thought I would do it for nothing," said the man.

"Oh no, brother, the laborer is worth his hire!" said Keith.

This man sat down and cried in Keith's living room. He was in his seventies and had done this kind of work all of his life. Men who should be the first to pay the laborer had taken advantage

of him. It's one thing to accept a gift from someone, but it's altogether wrong to take advantage of someone.

ESTEEMED THEMSELVES

In my vision the men in the circle esteemed themselves alone. They
sought for applause, cheers and attention from others. They are the
kind of people who want to be the bride at every wedding and the
corpse at every funeral. But the genuine leaders in Christ exalt and
care for the needs of their brothers and sisters. They have no desire
to be the center of attention, but every desire to build up fellow
believers (see Rom. 12:9-16; Phil. 2:1-11).

As apostle Mel Davis, overseer of International Association of
Ministers based in British Columbia, Canada, puts it:

> If I cannot esteem another brother, there's something wrong
> with me inside. The brothers that God uses have large spir-
> its. Ever notice how the men of God who God uses pow-
> erfully, react to another ministry? They will clap, applaud,
> amen, and compliment them with tears in their eyes, for the
> smallest things they do. Anything done in Christ's name is
> a joy to them and they delight in it, while those with small
> spirits and ineffective ministries will never compliment, or
> applaud another brother. They fail to realize that the way
> we esteem each other is the way we will be esteemed.

The men in the circle were also accountable to no one. The Bible
makes it clear that we need the physical and emotional strength from
others to stand (see Eccles. 4:9-12), but we need healthy accountability from other Christians for admonishment and growth too (see
Rom. 15:14; Eph. 4:16; Col. 3:15-17; 1 Thess. 5:12; Titus 2:15).
Pastor Jimmy Mas has this perspective on such leadership:

I don't have any respect for leaders who are unwilling to be confronted and accountable and I don't care how old or young they are, or how successful they've been—it means nothing. Why? Because people in the seats want principle and they want principle-oriented leadership.

Pastor Dion Boffo adds this about leadership and accountability:

> If the people in church see that the leader is not disciplined, they are not going to be disciplined. The leader can talk about principles, discipline, restoration and so forth, but if that is not taking place in his personal life, it's not going to take place in the church.
>
> One of the ways to find out if it's taking place in your personal life is to answer these questions: To whom are you accountable? Who is checking up on you? To whom have you given permission to check up on things in your life? Who have you given permission to ask how your prayer life is going? How is the wife? How are things going with your family? When we are talking about church discipline, we are talking about self-discipline, and developing those character qualities that are important in the Kingdom.

When you ask some church leaders about being accountable, they will say, "I'm accountable to my board." But in most cases, the board will not want to offend leadership and are not dependable for oversight. The leader hired the board and the leader can fire the board. We need someone who knows what is going on in our lives and is not worried about offending us—someone whom we can depend on to always give us an honest assessment. It's for our own good; otherwise we could end up like those who I saw in the circle casting their seed.

THE ANOINTING CAN BE DANGEROUS

Moreover, God's gifting a person does not make that person a minister. Joe Warner tells the story of a man who was incredibly gifted and because of his gifting, he was released into ministry by a network of churches. Because there were no fathers to watch over him, he destroyed six churches. He could do that because he had a great anointing; he had awesome teaching ability and was one of the best communicators Joe had ever heard.

Many men have great oratory ability, gifting and various skills, but have no functioning ministry. Peter was called to be a fisher of men, but after three and a half years, he was not yet fishing for men. When Christ rose from the dead and appeared to Peter, what was he fishing for? Fish! He had not yet begun fishing for men, although he had been called to do so.

The anointing can be dangerous if used improperly. The greater your sphere of influence and anointing, the more dangerous you become—not only to the enemy, but also to the kingdom of God. Because if you fail morally or spiritually, everything you have ever done in ministry becomes a joke. The greater your influence and anointing, the greater the need for a covering. I have five or six men that I know can be depended upon to speak into my life, but I've also asked Emanuele Cannistraci, senior pastor of Evangel Church in San Jose, California, to cover me and check on me. Those five or six may be a little hesitant to offend me, but I know that Emanuele isn't. He loves to offend me, so I know I can always depend on him.

If a home group leader starts a false doctrine, he can be corrected or he can be put out of the church. However, if the pastor starts a false doctrine, it could split the church, and he could gather a group to follow him. Leadership can be very dangerous to the Body of Christ, because if they stray, it can ruin many people. Leaders are more dangerous than the people sitting in the pews. This is why a pastor needs an apostle over him—not a superintendent! The pastor needs to be accountable to someone, in the same way his people have to be accountable to him.

VANITY OF THE FLESH

Now the Lord blew His trumpet and the Army of God got up and went back to their encampment. Then the Lord said to me, "Now, listen."

The soldiers were exclaiming to one another, "Man, we were attacked! We've been persecuted. What opposition! What warfare! We were tearing down strongholds. Now we can go have a breakthrough conference. Everyone will be changed from now on." And they began organizing breakthrough meetings and celebrating a victory such as had never before happened.

The people thought they had been on the battlefield, but they never had been.

The Warrior said, "They are mocked because of the vanity of their flesh and they interpret that as persecution."

I fell to my knees, saying, "God, I repent! I repent!"

The men who had been in the circle, casting their seed and cheering for those who could cast the farthest, were now back in their own fields giving glowing reports of great ministry efforts under the most difficult circumstances. They didn't realize that they had never even engaged the enemy. Nevertheless they told stories of great ministry and persecution for the sake of the gospel. They were deceived and even mocked because of the vanity of their flesh.

WALLS NEVER STOPPED BELIEVERS

Anyone who has ever ministered in Russia will tell you that in many ways, ministry in Russia was better before Communism was defeated. Now that the wall of Communism—the Iron Curtain—is down, there are all kinds of crazies going over there to minister. There are all kinds of weird people doing all kinds of weird things and bringing a multitude of bizarre ideas, strange doctrines and manifestations. That political wall never stopped believers from ministering in Russia; it only stopped the make-believers and professional ministers.

With opportunities opening up in China too, there are many believers in this country and in China who are concerned that the country will be affected by strange and false teachings. Timothy Wong (not his real name), an apostolic missionary from America to China, attended a Chinese consultation meeting in China that many Chinese apostles risked their lives to attend. Some of the greatest apostles in the world were right there – people who had oversight over thousands of churches in Red China. With tears in their eyes they begged Timothy, "Please, if the wall comes down, don't encourage Americans or other foreign ministers to come to China!"

These leaders made this appeal because they knew the kind of crazy things that would happen if foreign missionaries were allowed into China. They understood that a flood of strange teachings, distorted doctrines and manifestations would hurt the growth of the Kingdom in China. They were right to be concerned.

What a contrast to another American evangelist who was already planning to go into China. His plan was to raise money to buy 100,000 to 200,000 Bibles. With 10 percent of the money already raised, he was going to find 50 churches to help organize students who would then enter China with these Bibles. These students would then go out and sell the Bibles to the Chinese. He called that ministry.

That's strange. If he wanted to minister, why couldn't he do what Timothy Wong did—just get a visa and go to China? Timothy is there serving directly and imparting what he can and giving his life for the Chinese people. There is a wisdom with Wong that reflects commitment for growing the Kingdom. There is no government that can stop believers like Wong; there is no wall that can stop people of his caliber. Men and women of God will confront darkness in every corner of the earth.

CHAPTER SIX

WOUNDS FROM FOOLISH WARRIORS

GOING TO THE CROSS FOR HEALING AND FORGIVENESS

Speaking of the men spilling their seed, the Lord said to me, "My son, they know not what they do. Take your criticism and put it at the foot of the Cross, and you weep for these men. Cry for these men. Have compassion for these men. Have mercy for these men."

The Lord made it very clear that these men were not to be criticized. We are to weep, have compassion and mercy, and put our criticism at the foot of the Cross even though these men are often critical of any real move of God. The men in the circle are often-times powerful men with large ministries and churches. They are often gatekeepers in their cities, having great influence over what is accepted as "of God" and what is not. In the eyes of the world they are successful, but in the eyes of the discerning they are to be pitied and prayed for. If we don't follow the directive of the Lord and put our criticism at the foot of the Cross, we will become just like them.

The most painful wounds we will ever receive will come from those whom we thought were faithful brothers in the faith. There are many people in the Body of Christ who are offended, hurt and depressed because the ministry or the church has let them down. Sometimes we need help in dealing with our hurts in order that we might completely forgive those who may have wronged us. Unforgiveness is not an option for us. If we confess the sin in our lives, God is quick to forgive us, and we should forgive others.

Love is another requirement of the Christian—God demands it. We must show forgiveness and love toward our brothers and sisters. Love is something that we can't just claim; we must do it. Love is the ultimate quest that we work toward all our lives. We can't ever say that we "have it." This is the highest quest and the greatest test we will ever face in our spiritual walk. I believe the apostolic movement is really going to refine these two areas because these are areas that need it desperately. When we are in "love" we are in God. When we love our brother then we can say that we love our God (see 1 John 4:19,20). The world is not going to recognize Christians by our signs and wonders, but by the love we display (see John 13:34,35).

Pastor John Diana of Greater Pittsburgh Word and Worship had tens of thousands of dollars embezzled from his church by a person whom he thought was faithful. Included in what he stole was Pastor Diana's entire retirement fund; it was totally cleaned out. Pastor Diana says:

> The most important thing that was stolen was love and
> trust; someone whom I loved and trusted has stabbed
> me in the back. As I was driving down the road, I began
> to think about it and I got so angry that I began to cry.
> That's when the Lord spoke to me and said, "You are hurt
> much deeper and much worse than you realize and you
> need to get to a place where you can get some help."
>
> I went to the presbytery meeting of our elders, and
> I said, "Listen guys, I need ministry; I am wiped out
> over this thing." They poured the love of Christ into
> me. A healing process began, and I can honestly say
> I don't have a trace of anger toward this brother. I don't
> have a trace of animosity; I don't want the worst for
> him. I don't have evil thoughts; I really, honestly and
> truly want to see redemption and restoration take place
> in his life.

When a congregation witnesses this kind of forgiveness, it's
an encouragement to everyone and can take the whole church to
a new level of spirituality. We must not take lightly the admoni-
tion of the Lord:

> *Take your criticism and put it at the foot of the Cross and*
> *you weep for these men. Cry for these men. Have compassion*
> *for these men. Have mercy for these men.*

Sometimes when we see other ministers failing, we regard
them as competitors and are glad to see them fail. This is not
of God; every failure in the Body of Christ is a failure for us
because we are the Body of Christ. The men in the circle needed

healing the way pastor Diana needed healing, and it must come from the Body. Otherwise it won't work. Only the gentle ministry of the Holy Spirit can turn these men from their inward stance to where they can face outward and see God's bigger picture for them.

UNGODLY MIXTURE

The Lord continued, "This is a warning against mixing with nonvirile, nonproducing breeds; it is a warning against mixing incorruptible seed with corruptible seed. This is a warning for all the battalions in My kingdom."

In Romans 7:24, the apostle Paul said, "Who will rescue me from this body of death?" He was referring to a punishment given to enemy soldiers in ancient battles. When an especially strong and brave warrior was taken captive on the battlefield, he would be chained to a wall and have a dead body fastened to him. No matter how much they fed the captive, in a matter of days, death and disease would begin to enter his healthy body.

The Lord warned me against mixing with other breeds and mixing the incorruptible seed with the corruptible. He wants us to be careful of whom we are attached to in fellowship and partnership. There are many Christians today who are attached to a dead body—a spiritually dead relationship with someone or something (see 1 Cor. 15:33).

We hear many believers say, "I believe God has called me to witness to this church, or this denomination or this fellowship." However as we watch them over time, we can see their anointing dissipating. The vision they once had is no longer there. It is dying a slow death because the dead body to which they are attached is greater than they are, and it is having a greater influence on them than they are having on it. How many brothers and sisters do we know who have died ministerially because they are carrying dead weights? They're not even in the battle; they are simply in the circle or back at camp.

As Christians in a free society, we can become unified to any ministerial fellowship, church, group or organization we choose. But we should become unified to something that has vision and the life of Christ breathing in it rather than a burden of spiritual death attached. We should want to be part of something that has life in it so that there might be life in us.

God gave me Leviticus 19:19, and when I looked at it, I had very little comprehension until the Lord opened my spiritual eyes to what it meant. It says, "Do not mate different kinds of animals. Do not plant your field with two kinds of seed. Do not wear clothing woven of two kinds of material." God is trying to teach His people not to unify with just any person, fellowship, church or organization.

DO NOT MATE DIFFERENT KINDS OF ANIMALS.

The word "animals" in this passage can also be interpreted as "cattle." Moreover, what's being referred to here is a different kind of cattle—a special breed or a special bull. Do not allow yourself to be impregnated with inferior breeds. The meaning (type and shadow) of cattle in the Bible refers to people. The point of this Scripture is for us to be careful of whom we are linked or unified with in relationships and projects.

First Corinthians 9:9 says, "Do not muzzle an ox while it is treading out the grain." This obviously is referring to someone who is ministering the gospel; the context makes this apparent. When zeal is watered down, the gospel presentation is watered down. Leviticus 19:19 says that to prevent this, only unify (breed) with the strongest so that you won't be weakened by those with whom you are unified.

One of the greatest reasons for ministerial failure is a lack of mentors. In contrast, one of the greatest reasons for ministerial success is an abundance of mentors (see Prov. 11:14; 24:6). However, having many mentors from different persuasions is not the answer, but having many mentors with different giftings from the same persuasion is definitely the answer. When there are men of various persuasions speaking into our lives, there is confusion, double-mindedness and a dissipation of the anointing. But when men of common faith and vision come together, there is an increase of the anointing and ministry.

DO NOT PLANT YOUR FIELD WITH TWO KINDS OF SEED.

We should never plant two or more kinds of seeds in a field. It's logical that you would not want to plant tomatoes and cotton in the same field. The whole process of planting, nurturing and harvesting would be confused. Instead, you would plant one field with cotton and one with tomatoes and these distinct fields would allow for a speedy harvest. If you're in a climate that won't grow cotton, you wouldn't use that seed. The same is true in the spiritual realm. Paul told Timothy to choose specific men as deacons, and specific men as elders. He didn't say, "Just go out and get a bunch of volunteers." Paul knew the importance of planting with a certain kind of seed; that's why he said (referring to ordination) in 1 Timothy 5:22,

"Do not be hasty in the laying on of hands." The gospel is propagated and pollinated by what it plants.

DO NOT WEAR CLOTHING WOVEN OF TWO KINDS OF MATERIAL.

Clothing woven of linen and wool would tear apart in rainy weather. In the spiritual realm the same would be true if you were to receive from groups with competing agendas. Some folks think that more is better. They say, "I receive this from that group, and that from this group, and some from them." What happens then is that in crucial situations, they don't know from whom to receive and the whole thing falls apart. There is contraction when there should be expansion and expansion when there should be contraction. We need a spiritual covering that is stable. We can only have stability if we receive from and submit to one place.

In my vision the Lord said that this was "a warning." Do not mix with other breeds and do not mix incorruptible seed with corruptible seed. I have friends who raise cattle, and they would never use inferior bulls for breeding purposes. They are always thinking in terms of improving their herd, which inferior breeding would weaken. The same is true with the farmer: he would never use inferior seed (corruptible seed) because that would produce an inferior crop.

The Lord said in the vision to "cry for these men, have compassion for these men, have mercy for these men" because they were mixing with other breeds and mixing corruptible seed with the incorruptible seed. We are not to be critical of the men who were in the circle casting their seed, but we are to have compas-

sion on them. The Lord also said, "They know not what they do."
All of us must put our criticism at the foot of the Cross. Every
Christian's heart should be broken to see the Army of God in
such incredible confusion and error. We need to weep, fast and
pray for the Army of God.

There are times when we see these things happening and
there is nothing we can do. We can pray, fast and show mercy and
compassion, yet the confusion and error continue.

JUST BUILDING HOUSES

*I said to the Lord, "At least those ministers made an effort.
When the trumpet blew, they went over the hill."*

*The Warrior rebuked me, saying, "Are you thinking of
that small group in the distance?"*

*"Yes. When you blew the trumpet, that small group never
moved."*

*The Warrior said, "Would you like to see what they
were doing?"*

*"Certainly," I said, "because I would like to preach
against that kind of behavior." Then the Lord took me to
where the small group was waiting.*

*The Warrior said, "Watch!" He blew the trumpet and
the small group never moved. Suddenly they turned and
went backward.*

*I said, "I can't believe it; they're retreating on the day of
battle!"*

*In fact the group had set about building houses. At least the
other groups had made an effort to go to war; this group was
content to construct houses.*

In my hurry to judge I became indignant because the small group
was not making an effort to go into battle; in fact, it appeared as if

they were retreating. But God has always had His small group—held in reserve for the time of the real showdown—a small group that appeared to be all wrong, to be weird, to be out of the mainstream. That remnant is always the group that God will deal with and use.

On the day of Pentecost, 120 disciples were present. Where were all those Jesus had healed? Where were the thousands He fed? Where were the healed paralytics? Where were those he had set free from demons? Where were the many who followed Him as He traveled from place to place? Only a remnant remained; a small, insignificant, weird, weak bunch of outcasts. It seems incredible that of all the thousands Jesus ministered to during His lifetime, there were only 120 on the day of Pentecost.

Pastor Scott Loughrige of Crossroads Church and Ministries in Marshall, Michigan, teaches a concept called critical mass, which is a type of remnant in local church meetings. He says that there is a "people group" in all church meetings who are going to carry the meetings. If we come to church on Sunday morning and the first three songs are warm-up songs, you know whom I would hold responsible for that? The critical mass!

The critical mass can carry an event,

THERE IS NO SHORTAGE OF PEOPLE WHO WANT TO BUILD GOD'S KINGDOM, BUT THERE IS A SHORTAGE OF THE NECESSARY INGREDIENT THAT ALLOWS THEM TO BUILD EFFECTIVELY. THE NECESSARY INGREDIENT IS WISDOM.

because they're ready for worship, for evangelism and for teaching. In a room of 300 people, they are the 20 or 30 ready to praise the Lord. Don't expect the guy who just got saved last week to carry the meeting, because if he does, it's going to be terrible. The critical mass has the maturity to be vigilant and prepared in any circumstance to advance the Kingdom and people will be looking to them for leadership.

THE SMALL REMNANT OF WISE BUILDERS

Up to this point in my vision, everything was negative. I was beginning to think that there was no remedy, but that's foolish. God always has a remedy because He always has a remnant.

The small group was significant because they were building according to the pattern (though at the time I didn't realize it). In Christianity, there is no shortage of builders. Every nation, state, city, county, town, village, denomination and church group has folks who want to build something. They may want to build buildings for worship, recreation or study. Or maybe they have a desire to build something into people. There is no shortage of people who want to build, but there is a shortage of the necessary ingredient that allows them to build effectively. The necessary ingredient is *wisdom*.

Proverbs 9:1 says, "Wisdom has built her house." It is glaringly obvious that Christians have built many structures that can't and won't stand the test of time. The rains and storms—tests and trials—come, and the structure fails to stand. When the Bible speaks of building, it's referring to building our spiritual lives, not a stone edifice on the corner of Main Street.

The small group in my vision began building (spiritual) houses. Mel Davis says this about building the house of God:

Every house is built by some man; a wise man builds his house, his life, his ministry, on the Rock. When the rains come (the blessings of God), they come to the wise and the foolish. At times the wise and the foolish receive the blessings of God together. We are sometimes judged by our prosperity and blessing and unless we have integrity of character and the wisdom of God, we can be destroyed by blessings. I thank God for the moving of the wind and the moving of the Holy Spirit and the blessing of the Lord on our churches, but unless there is wisdom and understanding with this, it is going to produce strange manifestations and confusion.

Proverbs 24:3 says, "By wisdom a house is built." There is no substitute for wisdom in building the house of God. The foundational ministries for the building (see Eph. 2:20) are that of the apostle and the prophet. The prophet can speak the mind of God, but it takes the apostle to interpret and implement the building process. For many years we have heard that God was going to raise up apostles, but the apostles have always been here. What has been missing in many cases is the wisdom of the apostle.

According to Ephesians 4:11, the fivefold ministry is apostles, prophets, evangelists, pastors and teachers. I believe there are as many apostles as there are pastors, teachers, evangelists and prophets. There are apostolic leaders who operate as pastors, evangelists, prophets and teachers, and there are prophets who do the same. In fact most of the leaders who are pastoring today are not strictly pastors, but men whose main gift is something else. Every church, obviously, has a need for a pastor, but there is also the need for the other offices as well. Every church has a need for the prophetic gift—to hear the voice of the Lord—and there is a need for the teacher, evangelist and apostle. The ideal situation is where these gifts function together. We see this happening in mature churches, but the less mature congregations really struggle with this because they may have pastors and church leaders who are too insecure to want to see other gifts functioning. A mindset that wants all ministry to flow through one person hinders Kingdom building.

There is a difference between being apostolic and being an apostle; they are two separate things. There are individuals who function in an apostolic role and even know all the teachings concerning the apostle, but they don't have the anointing of the apostle. A person may be an apostolic teacher who can teach about the Church, or an apostolic prophet who sees the need for God's government in the church. These leaders are apostolic in ministry, not apostles in nature, because they lack the anointing to build. There are two reasons that some evangelists are apostolic: (1) they see the need to equip the local church, and (2) they will do church-planting crusades.

When I began my ministry, I was purely an evangelist; then I began to move into the prophetic ministry. The Lord then challenged me to build a church and from there I went into the apostolic. I believe I functioned in an apostolic role for a minimum of 10 years before I could say I was an apostle. It was not a goal of mine to operate as an apostle; it just happened. Only sons can promote a father, and as I functioned in the ministry, this is the title they gave to me. We never look for titles to put on folks; people function where the Lord puts them and eventually someone will give them a title.

The foundational ministry of the apostle is service (see Eph. 2:20). Paul said in 1 Corinthians 4:9, "God has put the apostles on display at the end of the procession." The apostle is a foundational ministry that puts it at the bottom, and it's the apostle who is at the end of the procession. What does this tell us about the apostolic ministry? We're servants! This is what the Lord called me to do when He said to me, "Go wash the feet of the young men who would be the patriarchs of the end-time move of my Spirit." Because God was gracious to me in spelling out what my calling is, I have no confusion about what I'm to do. Pastor David Cannistraci of Evangel Church in San Jose, California, has this to say about the apostle:

> Apostles are builders. The primary task of apostles, apostolic people, apostolic churches and networks is to build something for God. Apostles take a field that is barren, overgrown and filled with rocks and trash, and they clear the land. They pull the rocks out and plow it up, and pretty soon, where there was nothing, something gets planted, and in due season we reap, if we faint not. The apostle starts with nothing, but then plants and soon there is fruit. An apostle takes a parcel of land where there is no building and he surveys it; he looks it over; he grades it; lays a foundation; and then a super structure goes up, so that where there was nothing, now there is something. This is the function of an apostle—to build and plant for God. Building something from nothing is the mark of true apostleship.

I see the apostle as the coach or the quarterback of a football team. Actually the apostle is part coach and part quarterback. Sometimes the apostle has to be on the sidelines calling in the plays and instructing the players; at other times he's in the battle taking the hits himself and advancing his team against the enemy.

I like what Jack Kemp (former NFL quarterback, former

Congressman, former secretary of HUD and former vice-presidential candidate for the GOP) said about being a quarterback as quoted in *USA Today*:

> Everything a quarterback does involves cost-benefit decisions, risk-reward ratios, and marginal analysis. All decisions are quantifiable and measurable. You get 20 seconds to call the play, three seconds to get the ball off. The play either works or fails; the team either moves forward or is stopped; and the fans are with you—win or tie.

I never had the good fortune of playing quarterback (they always put the "big uglies" on the line), but what Jack says about it sounds very much like the way I sometimes feel about the apostle. The apostle, using wisdom, must make measurable advances for the kingdom of God. It may not be measurable to us, but God is keeping score.

Using that same football analogy, there are also tackles, guards, ends, linebackers, centers, running backs, defensive backs, water boys, trainers, doctors, etc., who are apostolic. I believe that a true apostolic network will have a plurality of apostles with various functions.

On a football team there are various positions that have to do with size, strength and speed. The same is true with the apostolic—there are various sizes, speeds and strengths. What God is trying to do is to match us up against the kingdom of darkness. In the Spirit the apostle will be able to see where a person belongs, and what evil spirit will be against that person.

There are various kinds of apostles in the Church today who can function only in certain situations. For example, I would not recommend some missionary apostles going into certain churches, because they may not be successful there. There are prophets who are apostolic and apostles who are prophetic. There are apostles who have a general apostolic ministry because they think governmentally and strategically for building the local church and building ministries and for getting everyone in their proper place (for the purpose of warfare).

A big problem in ministry is those ministers who would put themselves in a position of failure because they see themselves as being higher than they are. They may envision themselves pastoring a big church in a big city; consequently they go to a geographical area of big churches and wind up with the smallest church in town. There are pastors in the city who should be pastoring in the country. Some traveling ministers have to be honest with themselves and realize that they have a small-church ministry while others may have a big-church ministry. There is nothing wrong or less important about having a small-church ministry; it is needed. If we don't realize God's placement of our ministry, we will experience frustration and disappointment.

I've also seen pastors put other believers in a position of failure. The pastor whose motor was running at 120 mph convinced someone working with him that he had to run at the same speed. In reality, that person's speed was 60 mph. Running at a speed a person isn't designed for by God leads to failure.

IN THE RIGHT APOSTOLIC POSITION

In the Church today there are many apostolic ministers (not necessarily apostles) serving as pastors, prophets, evangelists or teachers. In an apostolic network, you will find these apostolic leaders—a proliferation of ministers performing many functions.

James Jorgensen was raised in a church in Brooklyn, New York, but he wasn't sent to do warfare there. He was sent to the

Dominican Republic to do warfare as a prophet with an apostolic understanding. In the Dominican Republic, he ministered alongside national apostles with a general's ministry; when the prophetic apostolic brother joins with the general apostolic brother, there is great success in ministry.

Apostle Joe Mattera of Resurrection Church, who is also from Brooklyn has a strong prophetic ministry. He has a dynamic apostolic understanding and an emerging apostolic anointing. When he goes to the Dominican Republic, he brings another level of assistance. When he leaves, apostle Gary Gonzalez (whose gifts have matured from evangelist to prophetic evangelist with an apostolic anointing) comes in. All these men work in the harvest field side by side, using the gifts the Lord has given them for building the kingdom of God.

There are apostolic teachers who can train leaders and give a theology and a blueprint to apostles throughout the world. There are even church planters who are not apostles by title but are in apostolic work.

God wants to match up the right people with the right positions.

APOSTLES ARE DEVELOPED

The "New Apostolic Reformation" is a term that was first used by C. Peter Wagner. Peter is a missiologist, church-growth expert, author and professor (Fuller Theological Seminary) who is well known throughout the Evangelical community. He has gone through a transformation from being in a very strict Evangelical camp to becoming a Spirit-filled man who believes in miracles, healing, spiritual warfare, etc. He arrived at his present conclusion by his academic study and observation that the Church will never be what it is called to until there is a restoration of apostles.

Apostles are developed. Very much like the pastor, teacher or prophet, they must first go through much learning and development. The process for apostles, however, is much more intense, for they must put away all self-ambition and be committed to the success of others.

In Zechariah 3:1–2, Joshua the high priest is standing before the angel of the Lord and Satan. Joshua was a restoration prophet; Nehemiah and the other prophets are there to anoint him as the high priest over the new city of Jerusalem. Satan is there to accuse Joshua. The Lord says to Satan, "Is not this man a burning stick snatched from the fire?"

The worst thing that can happen to any minister is to be an overnight success! Every man and woman of God must go through wilderness in order to be truly prepared for ministry. It was in the wilderness that Jesus was tempted and tested (see Matt. 4:1-11) and it was in the wilderness that Paul came to grips with his destiny, anointing and calling (see 2 Cor. 11:23-29). Those who have been through the wilderness are sick and tired of wandering. They will cross the Jordan at all costs. It doesn't matter what giants are in the land; it doesn't matter what Satan says or does. The fire-tested minister will take his destiny because he or she was tested in the wilderness and the fire has forged him or her for the purposes of God.

When I was a boy my whole family were structural iron workers: father, uncles, cousins and grandfathers. At 16 I went to work as a steel worker. I'll never forget my first day on the job; it was frightening. I didn't know how to walk on the steel, the thought of which was intimidating. Clyde Cree, a Mohawk Indian who worked in the steel mill with me, gave me advice that I've never forgotten. He said, "In order to walk in the sky, you first have to know how to walk on the earth." When you walk on steel, high above the traffic or river below, you have to look where you're going, not at your feet or what's below. You have to keep your eyes focused on your goal and never flinch. If you're looking at your feet (self) or what's below, you will fall. In the ministry the principle is the same: Walk toward the goal, the throne of God, and raise up the Church to its manifest destiny in order that Jesus may rule and reign on the earth.

GOD DOESN'T LOOK AT THE FLESH

Gary Kivelowitz is a common case of how the Lord can use and develop a man into a minister. When I first met Gary, he was so shy that if we were in a group of people, he wouldn't talk to anyone. In order to try to bring Gary out of this, I would prod him to go and talk to someone. He would ask me, "What should I say?"

I would tell him, "Go and introduce yourself."

He would go and introduce himself and come back and ask me, "What should I say now?"

Today Gary is an articulate, all-purpose minister whom God is using to strengthen men. Gary's development is a marvelous case of what God can do if we allow Him. There is nothing mystical about his development or his ministry. He developed in a normal way and is now used of God to impart to others.

HEALTHY AND UNHEALTHY MIND-SETS

Many believers tend to think of the apostle as an out-of-this-world, surreal mystic, and to a larger degree people even perceive the Body of Christ as an ethereal institution. But there is nothing cosmic, bizarre or grandiose about being an apostle or about the Body of Christ.

In fact, I often view the apostle as a glorified counselor. It is not a glamorous position, but it is the ministry that must serve all others. The ministry of an apostle is down-to-earth, sensible, practical and designed to plant, build up and release people into the places they belong—the ministries to which God calls them. The role of the apostle can, to some degree, minister within the operation of other ministry gifts—pastor, teacher, evangelist and prophet. The apostle is a practical builder.

I see the Body of Christ like a net that is visible and touchable. Christians form this net and the purpose of it is to catch people and bring them into the Kingdom (see Matt. 13:47). However, the majority of apostolic networks operate mystically—the leader is not sensible or practical—but sort of an untouchable, never-wrong, "God's chosen" instrument. Under such domination, a ministry is transformed into a personal vehicle for control. Such "apostles" have hidden ungodly agendas as they influence people. They like to be in control and have the corner on God's revelation that keeps everyone else, with the exception of a select few, in the dark.

In my opinion, there are three kinds of unhealthy mind-sets found in some apostles today:

1. The Wounded Heart

This apostolic leader is a person who has been hurt. These hurts may be legitimate and may have happened under some kind of previous abusive leadership. Deep insecurities drive this person to resist commitment to others.

2. The Controlling Nature

This person can be petty and bring a ministry to analytical paralysis. Everything has to be overdefined and an inordinate amount of emphasis is placed on minor issues, small variations in words, tiny changes in appearance and style. The ministry degenerates into nitpickers because the leadership is always trying to define who and what they are.

3. The Ignorant Mind

This leader simply has no understanding of the government of God, no matter how hard he tries to understand God's pattern for Church organization. Often his personal dysfunction in relationships or marriage hinders him from acting in wisdom. He may have a problem with male headship, because he can't figure out who is to be the head in the house, and that carries over into the Church.

Unfortunately, due to poor leadership, many apostolic networks (parachurch ministries that operate in and coordinate efforts with churches that accept the fivefold ministry of apostle, prophet, evangelist, pastor and teacher) become environments that emotionally and spiritually wound believers associated with them.

APPROPRIATE APOSTOLIC AUTHORITY

There are some apostolic ministries that believe their authority reaches all the way into the local church. But the apostolic network should never penetrate the veil of the local church—the local, everyday affairs—unless the pastor is exhibiting immoral behavior or teaching heresy. In those instances, the apostolic network should step in and bring healing to the situation.

This type of governmental authority is a reproduction of the Roman Catholic Church with the Pope at the head, having authority over every pastor, church member and church.

Most apostolic ministries want to have authority in the local church, but I believe that the local church should be self-governed. The spiritual authority of an apostolic ministry should not go beyond the pastor; the pastor is the authority over the local church. Why would we want authority beyond that? Is there a desire to control? The more control we have the smaller the thing we will build and the less effective it will be. Our intellect is limited and so is our ability to manage. But if we build through relationship and influence, we can accomplish much more in building the Kingdom.

ROLE OF THE APOSTLE

I see my role as an apostle. I stand and bridge the gap between missions outreach and churches so they can build together. Also, I stand between individual churches and bring them together. One church of 100, 200 or 300 people is limited in taking a city or region, but when they are joined by covenant they are far stronger. Another role is to provide apostolic pastors for pastors, and apostolic church planters for church planters so there might be leadership development, plans and strategies for building the kingdom of God beyond my own generation.

The role of an apostle always forces self-examination. I believe the heart is of far greater importance than the mind because the all-important question is: What is our motivation? Do we need attention or control? Do we have a need to say that there are men and churches "under" us?

I have no churches or missions "under" me, and I'm quite content because I know that no churches or missions belong "under" me. If I had a bunch of churches and missions to control, my life span would be shortened. My role is to help other believers release what God has given them and to teach and empower others individually and corporately to build God's kingdom. This is not an easy thing to do.

Many believers struggle with being spiritual sons. It's generally in our nature to rebel against a father; nearly everyone goes

IF WE HOLD

ON TOO

TIGHTLY

TO OUR

SPIRITUAL

CHILDREN,

WE RISK

CRUSHING

THE

OPPORTUNITY FOR

THEIR FAITH

TO BECOME

PERSONALIZED—

TO BE THEIR

FAITH.

through it. The son will go through a period of dependence but when he becomes a teenager, he wants to be totally independent of oversight.

During this time a spiritual father may be rejected, but the father must be wise enough to fight the temptation to hold on too tightly. Every spiritual son we have is based on a decision similar to how each of us decides to become a son of God. We make a decision to be part of God's family, but we can rebel at any time. The amazing thing is that God allows it. Eventually a spiritual son will reach maturity, and when that happens he will make the decision to be interdependent with the spiritual father.

Yes, I believe in sound structure for Church operations, and in accountability, and in commitment to one another, but I also believe in giving some measure of freedom to our spiritual offspring. The reason is simple: The time when they are stretching themselves, testing the waters with us, is the time they are transitioning from childhood into maturity. Those must be their decisions – not our will imposed on them. If we hold on too tightly to our spiritual children, we risk crushing the opportunity for their faith to become personalized—to be *their* faith.

WOUNDS FROM FOOLISH WARRIORS   117

There have been a couple times in my apostolic ministry when men would say that I was giving a certain son too much rope; my reply to that is, "No, I was just seeing what was really there." You don't know what is in the heart of a son as long as you're giving orders. When you stop giving the orders, you discover what is really inside the heart, because that son must act on some things independently and the decisions reflect the character that the father has nurtured.

It comes down to this: The difference between God's Army and man's army is that man's army is held together by fear and punishment while God's Army is held together by love and covenant.

WHAT DO WE TEACH AND HOW DO WE FUNCTION?

A number of years ago I was speaking in a church that had about 200 to 250 members, and about 14 elders. These elders had taught on the fivefold ministry (see Eph. 4:11) of apostles, prophets, evangelists, pastors and teachers for about 15 years. This church was next to a major university and most of the elders were university professors. During a meeting with the elders, we had a question and answer session, with them questioning me on the validity of an apostolic network. They seemed to agree on everything that I had to say and were very affirming. However, I sensed that like most churches, they were giving lip service to certain things, but weren't functioning in those things.

When we broke for lunch, I asked the youth pastor to bring me a blackboard when we resumed our meeting after lunch. After lunch, when we were about to resume our meeting, in came the youth pastor with a blackboard.

I said to the elders, "During this afternoon meeting, I would like to ask you some questions. Why is it that after 15 years of teaching on the fivefold ministry, plurality of elders and raising up the Body of Christ to maturity, you aren't functioning in these things?"

One of the elders responded by saying, "We do! Here we are. We're the proof."

"No, you don't prove anything, and furthermore, you are not an apostolic church," I responded.

I then went to the blackboard that the youth pastor had brought into the meeting, and I wrote five words on it: "vision," "government," "doctrine," "accountability" and "involvement."

Then I said, "Gentlemen, this is what I propose. I will give this church $5,000 if you can: First, show me that the missions or missionaries you support have the same vision of the Kingdom and put it first as far as ruling and reigning over nations, powers, and principalities (a victorious church at war). Second, show me that the missions or missionaries that this church supports believe in the definition of God's government and function in it. Third, show me any mission or missionary that believes doctrinally as you do. (I don't mean in salvation or water baptism, the obvious things, but what I mean is the doctrine of the kingdom of God and the doctrine of the Church.) Fourth, show me one mission or missionary with a real sense of accountability; one that gives you a report on financial or relational accountability. (It doesn't have to be governmental accountability.) And fifth, could you recommend this mission or missionary for any saint in your church to get involved with?"

As I expected, the elders looked puzzled. They went to their missions map and after two and a half hours of discussing and arguing they said, "Well, this fellow believes exactly as we do."

I said, "Yes, but does he function in what he says he believes?"

"Oh!" they responded.

Then I said, "I'll tell you what, just give me one mission or missionary that functions in vision and government as you do, and you can pick any one of the other three criteria, and I will still give you the $5,000."

This time it only took an hour and a half of arguing and discussing, but they still came to the same decision that they knew of no mission or missionary they supported that had the same beliefs as they did and functioned in them.

This scenario exists in many churches today. Local churches have a tendency to say, "This is what we believe in," but function in a completely different way.

RESTORE ALL THINGS

Acts 3:21 says, "He must remain in heaven until the time comes for God to restore everything, as he promised long ago through his holy prophets." After the first century, the Church was on a steady decline in power and influence, until the fifteenth century when God began to restore it. Today the Church is having the greatest period of restoration it has ever experienced. There are more saints on earth today than all the saints combined throughout history. Revivals are going on all over the earth (Latin America, South America, Korea, China, etc.), and thousands are being saved every day.

It will be impossible for a church to move into the apostolic reformation and fulfill its destiny unless it is with like-minded churches. The new apostolic order is going to create the courage in us to make us able to step out of the old Church and become the new Church that God has destined us to be.

Just as that little group I saw in my vision were not just building, but building according to the biblical pattern, so ought we to be. They were a small group, but they were effective where the much larger group was totally ineffective.

CHAPTER SEVEN

RECRUITING WARRIORS

KNOWING THE RANGE OF AUTHORITY IN PLANTING AND HELPING CHURCHES

The Warrior said to me, "Watch this!" He blew the trumpet and out of the houses came young warriors. Again He blew the trumpet and the young warriors turned around and built houses themselves.

Again He blew the trumpet and out of the new houses came younger warriors. He blew the trumpet again and the younger warriors built houses. He blew the trumpet again and out of the houses came even younger warriors.

Then He said, "Come back with Me as I blow the trumpet again."

Frustrated, I said, "Wait a minute, Warrior, what's wrong with these ministers? When the trumpet blows they turn around and build houses."

"They are properly discerning the sound of the trumpet," the Warrior explained. "For they are building My habita-

*tion. They are building My house. Shall we go back there
again since you did not properly discern this yourself?"*
    "Yes," I said, chagrined.

The small group of warriors had been preparing for battle and
doing battle in the best possible way—building! This group was
the only group that properly discerned the trumpet call of God;
the trumpet was a clarion call to all of Christianity to build. The
small group responded by investing their lives in the next generation. Consequently, every generation was getting stronger than
the previous one. The sons were getting stronger because the
fathers were stronger, and the fathers were doing a better job of
imparting life to their sons.

    The majority of men in ministry today have never been
fathered. This is one reason they have such a difficult time fathering anyone else. When men are raised up in the church and are
not fathered, either through neglect or inability, they have little or
no ability to father someone else.

    The men in the circle who were casting their seed inward were
not producing spiritual offspring. There was an inability and/or
neglect on their part, because they had their own agendas. Their
focus was inward and not on building into others. They were not
investing in the next generation. Perhaps no one had ever poured
his life into them. When ministers build according to a personal
agenda, it can never be called an apostolic work.

    A true apostolic work will always build according to the
biblical pattern. Just because there needs to be a restoration of
the apostolic ministry, doesn't mean that the apostles have been
absent altogether. The small group in my vision was apostolic.
I know this because of what they were doing—building and
producing spiritual children. The small group was not looking
inward nor serving their own agendas; they were serving the big-

ger picture by building the Kingdom into the next generation—warriors who would take the mantle and defeat the enemy.

I saw in the vision that the small group had been on the scene for many generations (God always has His remnant) because they produced many generations of sons. They could discern the trumpet call of God because they had ears to hear what the Spirit is saying to the Church. This call is the same call that has resonated throughout the ages—build! Only a remnant has heard and only a remnant has responded, but I can see where the response to God's call will multiply in the coming days.

A person with an anointing and a plan can plant a church, but that doesn't mean that they're building. Proper building must be done according to the biblical pattern. Years ago I planted churches for a Pentecostal denomination. I was anointed and had a plan; therefore, I had no trouble planting four churches of 200 people over a four-year period. Another man and I were on an experimental team. He had a pastoral gift, I was the evangelist-prophet, and we would set up as many meetings for women as we could. We would have day and evening meetings and eventually we grew to having meetings every day of the week. When we reached that number of meetings, we would call our first church service.

Our goal was to have 100 people at the first service as well as maintaining our daily meetings. At first we didn't have any male home-group leaders. But once we started the church, we would begin training men to be what we called care-leaders, and the men would start taking over some of the groups.

We would keep the daytime women's meetings going. On some days we would have two meetings—morning and evening and sometimes in the afternoon. Women would not conduct the meetings, but the women were tremendous at gathering people. We would do a lot of teaching and during ministry time I would prophesy over them. In 12 months we would be up to 200 people with about $10,000 in the building fund. That's when the denomination would bring in a pastor to take over the church.

If I were planting a church today, I would use the same plan. The only difference would be that I would implement a New Testament government. Women are the ones to focus on when planting a church; the men will eventually come. When Jesus speaks with the woman at the well in John 4:7-30, verses 28-30 tell us, "The woman went back to the town and said to the people, 'Come, see a man who told me everything I ever did. Could this be the Christ?' They came out of the town and made their way toward him." We based our strategy on this Scripture and it worked extremely well for us.

THE POWER OF COACHING

I love to coach warriors, and warriors love to be coached. When I go to Florida to visit Pastor Jimmy Mas, he'll let me stretch out on his couch and he'll get me a Diet Coke and say, "Okay, Papa, give it to me. You won't hurt my feelings." He wants me to suggest corrections that I think are appropriate in how he is Kingdom building. Usually there is nothing that needs major adjusting, but the fact that he is willing to receive shows me the heart of a genuine warrior for Christ.

Authentic warriors never say, "Hey, I've tried that, been there, done that and read the book." Real warriors thrive on being coached. I learned many years ago the importance of being coached; it practically saved my life and taught me a lesson I would never forget.

The sixth grade was a pivotal time of growing up. So much happened to me. I was put in a special education class; I was very shy, a loner, and often mocked by the other kids because I had trouble reading. I also had a hormone problem and wasn't growing right, and because of asthma I couldn't play sports.

During this difficult time three people came into my life who encouraged and coached me to better myself. In each instance, it was tough in the beginning because I had to overcome obstacles, but the results were tremendous for me.

First, I had a great teacher who believed in me. Her name was Mrs. Imhoff. She said to me, "John Kelly, you're smart and you're going to learn how to read!" She kept me after school every day for two hours teaching me how to read. The results in my life were incredible. When I graduated from sixth grade, Mrs. Imhoff had brought me up to the sixth-grade reading level. I was only a C student, but at least I was reading at the right grade level. Because of Mrs. Imhoff's teaching (coaching), something happened to me internally. I changed and began to think, *Man, I can read!* The high point came when I graduated magna cum laude from the eighth grade two years later.

While I was learning to improve my reading at school, another event also affected my reading ability. It started with my dad and our next door neighbor, Mr. Smantana (a scientist who had done some work on the atomic bomb). They were having one of their casual conversations when Mr. Smantana said to my dad, "You ought to have a Cadillac, Kelly!"

My dad replied, "You're right!"

The next thing I knew, there were six junk Cadillacs in our two yards. They set out to put together two Cadillacs out of the wrecks they bought from the junkyard. It gets better. Every day as they worked on the cars they would have me read the car manual to them. Now, that was a time when I could barely read. Yet every day I was reading this technical stuff that was way over my head.

Around that time Mr. Smantana said something to me that greatly affected my life. He said, "John, if you know how to read, there's nothing you can't do. This book is all about the parts of a Cadillac and because of this book, your daddy and I will have brand-new Cadillacs at the end of the year." He was right. At the end of that year, Mr. Smantana and my father had brand-new Cadillacs because they used information in a book that I read to them.

The third impact came with my doctor. He took an interest in me and introduced me to his son who was a weight lifter. His son encouraged me to lift weights with him, and his coaching helped me turn fat into muscle. The effects of this training made my lungs expand and made my asthma go away to the point where I eventually could play freshman football. I made the varsity team as a freshman and even made the all-county team. Suddenly I found myself a star. I was amazed because the previous year the other kids had laughed at me and teased me. The guys would say to the girls at school, "See fat, dumb Kelly? That's going to be your boyfriend." Imagine how surprised they were at my transformation!

All these growing positive results happened through mentoring. I had a teacher who loved me enough to teach me how to read. I changed because my father and his friend asked me to read a car manual, which showed me that reading books could empower me to build and obtain goals. I became an athlete because a doctor and his son encouraged me to improve myself physically. I was the kind of kid who always listened to my coaches because I believed – and still believe – that listening is the key to success.

Therefore, when I started boxing, it was natural for me to do whatever I was told. In my 77 career fights, I never won the first round; I got beaten up every time. I would sweat so badly that I couldn't see, so my coach would holler for me to throw my overhand right. I had two things to my advantage: I had a great coach and a great overhand right. There were guys bigger and tougher, but because of the length of my body (I guess), I had a great overhand right. When my coach would see my opponent drop his guard, he would holler for me to throw my right and I would. This is what coaching is all about – doing the right thing at the right time.

Because of these experiences in my youth, I believe in the tremendous impact a coach—mentor, teacher, counselor—can have on a young person. The small group I saw in my vision was obviously successful in coaching because they were producing sons who were growing in stature with every passing generation. But the group of ministers who were in the circle facing inward, instead of producing sons, were saying, "It's my ministry and it's my church." This stops the reproduction and virility of sons, and the attitude of "my church" becomes a spiritual prophylactic that will stop the seed that was planted by God. Instead of producing sons, they produce orphans and bastards.

SONS IN THE HOUSE

Another important aspect of the vision is that the sons were raised *in* the house. The house in this case means the local community of believers—not a physical structure, but the family of God as expressed in the *local community*.

The Church at Antioch believed in

WHEN A MINISTER SAYS, "IT'S MY MINISTRY AND IT'S MY CHURCH," HE STOPS THE REPRODUCTION AND VIRILITY OF SPIRITUAL SONS.

the reproduction principle and reproduced itself many times over. They reproduced by sending sons to plant churches. When Moses wanted to send a leader into the Promised Land, He sent Joshua; when the Father wanted to bring salvation to planet Earth, He sent His Son Jesus and not an angel (messenger). He sent a Son who was faithful in His house. A man who has been raised in the house can handle the things concerning the house.

This contrasts sharply with people who are messengers—those who haven't been raised in the local community of believers where they've been commissioned to raise up a new church. These messengers may even have gone to Bible school or seminary (there is nothing wrong with that), but if the person isn't a true son, raised in the house (that local community), he is destined for trouble.

The only way the messenger can come into some form of sonship is to have a spiritual father adopt him. A bona fide spiritual father adds enormous insight and encouragement to the local community's needs and to God's government for the Church.

PLANT WITH SONS

A key to church planting is sending a son who has been raised in the local church and is under a spiritual father; when he goes to plant a church, he is already relating to an apostolic man who can mentor him in the planting process.

An example of this occurred a couple of years ago when a simple problem arose involving a pastor in a local church. Although this pastor was part of our network, he had the wrong perception of authority. He was a person with some hurt in his life from abuse in a shepherding movement. He thought that the leaders in ACM wanted to control him as a previous movement had done. He was afraid that the problems in his church would move us to take him out of the ministry.

I sent someone to explain to the pastor that we didn't operate by micromanagement or instantly replacing someone for a mistake. We were there to minister, encourage, admonish and to make his efforts stronger. I also sent this representative to help the pastor take care of this minor problem in the church. The messenger went and explained the situation to the pastor, but the problem persisted. Then, I sent someone else to explain the situation to the pastor. He did, but the problem persisted. Finally I sent another person and the issue went away almost immediately.

What happened? The first two guys said the same thing as the third guy. Then it dawned on me! I had sent a messenger when I should have sent a son brought up in the house! The messenger could tell the truth and could lay out all the details, but he could not convey the heart of it. He could not convey the heart of the father. The same thing must be done in a church plant. The heart of the Father must be conveyed, and not just some plan or strategy. The man sent to plant a church must have the heart and spirit of the heavenly Father in order to plant properly.

CHURCH PLANTING GIFTS

As long as the person sent to plant a new church is a son of the local community of believers, there is a greater degree of success, regardless of what his ministry gift may be. But some gifts do prove more effective than others in church planting at different points of the church-growth process.

I am convinced that a big mistake we make in church planting is to begin with someone gifted in pastoring. These men want to go in and coddle people from the start. The pastor will begin to draw people into a group and he'll get fixated on that group and inadvertently fail to build up momentum for greater numbers to attend.

In the beginning, the best men to send to plant a church are the evangelists, prophets and apostles. The evangelist can go into a new area, win souls and begin to draw a crowd with that anointing. The prophet is effective in planting churches because he can go into an area and birth a crowd—especially in America—by speaking the prophetic word. Both the evangelist and prophet seem to operate best when they can raise the new church up to about 200 people, and then hand it over to the pastor who will shepherd continued growth.

Though the prophet and evangelist are the best at planting a church, after about the third year they start to dislike the crowd, and the crowd is tired of "getting saved" every Sunday. With the prophet the people will get tired of hearing prophecies spoken over them. How many times can you be prophesied over before it becomes old and worn? That is why it is critical for the pastor to come in at this point in the process.

The apostle has a similar effect on a new church as the evangelist and prophet. The main difference is that the apostle seems to nurture and attract larger numbers of people early on because of his ability to network. The apostle, however, should also allow the pastor to eventually come in to cultivate growth and maturity among the brethren.

APOSTOLIC AUTHORITY AND THE HOUSE

In the vision, the sons were being nurtured in the "house"—this is the spiritual sphere of authority commonly seen as the local community of believers. This is an important observation. The apostle has a certain sphere of spiritual authority, but his authority doesn't extend everywhere. There is a principle of spiritual authority related to the "house."

Nearly everyone has a sphere where they are in authority. Granted, in some cases that authority is very limited. For example, our Antioch network conference would be considered my sphere of authority, my local "house," and those who attend the event should have an attitude of submission. However, at another group's conference or at a local church, my role would be to submit to the local leader there—it's his sphere of authority, his house to watch over. It doesn't matter how large an apostolic ministry is; the role of an apostle is always to serve.

A PRINCIPLE OF THE HOUSE

When I go to the local church, I am in the pastor's "house" and I am a visitor, a guest. I am not there to violate anything that is under his care. I would not violate his family, elders or flock—those are all people under his sphere of authority. I would be there to submit and serve. However, the dynamics of authority change when the pastor is not with his congregation or family. When I'm alone with him or any brother who is committed to our network, he is back in my "house"—my sphere of authority.

We have to know when we are going in and coming out of someone's "house" and that situation can change rapidly. If I'm visiting a pastor and ministering in his church, he is the man of the house and I would submit to him. If I were training him in the apostolic, when we're alone, he hands the authority back to me. But if we suddenly get together with his leaders, I would then return the authority to him.

Men who can't do that will never successfully minister as apostles, and if they have networks, the networks will eventually break. It was for this reason I was able to predict the breakup of four apostolic networks – because there was no understanding of how authority operates in each house. It doesn't take a prophet to predict that.

INTEGRITY

Apostolic anointing and apostolic know-how are very important, but a lack of integrity can erase all that. We must understand something about the anointing. There are two seductions that come with it:

Power seduction

This temptation grows as crowds of people are drawn to your leadership. It's easy to find yourself thinking that all of God's plans and counsel come from you alone. Pride often overtakes us subtly and makes us unwilling to hear correction (see Prov. 16:18).

Sexual seduction

When you have a powerful anointing, people of the opposite sex become attracted to you. You could have an ugly physical appearance, but they would still be drawn to your presence. Unless you show wisdom in interacting with people, you can become ensnared through this temptation (see Jas. 1:14,15).

An apostle must have integrity when going into another person's house. If an apostle hungers for compliments and flattering responses to his ministry, he is close to danger. The Scriptures give sober warnings about how to receive and take praise from others:

> The crucible for silver and the furnace for gold, but man is tested by the praise he receives. Whoever flatters his neighbor is spreading a net for his feet (Prov. 27:21; 29:5).

As apostles we must keep our hearts in check; we could unintentionally draw the sons out of our brother's house and hurt his efforts. There must be integrity in any conversations with the sons of that house. We must also maintain honesty with the father of that house about what is in the conversations with the sons.

For instance, there may be a son who is going through an independent stage. He may come to me and say, "You're much more anointed than our pastor." You have to be careful with such a statement. Moreover, no matter how much you agree or disagree with the flattery (flatterers have a hidden agenda) keep in mind that flattery leads to death (see Pss. 5:9; 12:2,3; Prov. 26:28). I try to make the fathers of a ministry privy to the conversations I have with the sons—everything is out on the table—even if the son gives a negative comment about his spiritual father...a comment that may have validity and one that I agree with.

HONOR THE LEADER

Another principle I follow is to honor the father of the "house." The Scriptures say, "Be devoted to one another in brotherly love. Honor one another above yourselves" (Rom. 12:10). I especially try to let people know how I feel about the man who is over that house. When I go to a house, I am there to serve him, not his sons. Some would have a problem with this, but I'm not in that house to serve his sons because that is his responsibility.

Some apostles make this mistake: They go to another man's house with a natural father's heart—the desire to nurture, wanting to build up the sons. There is nothing wrong with this attitude, but the more you go with the heart of a natural father, the more likely you'll have problems with the leader. This is because you will try to be a father to his sons; you may not even know that you are wooing his sons away, that you are stealing their hearts from the father of that ministry or congregation. This is where a lot of traveling ministry leaders go wrong. Instead of serving the father, they end up wooing his sons.

DISCERNING THE SOUND OF THE TRUMPET

I finally realized that this small group of people in the vision were building God's kingdom in a proper fashion. I didn't realize this at first. I thought they were like so many groups I see today who build without using biblical principles rooted in godly authority, biblical organization, spiritual planting and cultivation of holiness, humility and forgiveness. The Church needs to recognize what God's pattern and principles are for Church government and growth.

Wood, hay and stubble cannot build the house of God (see 1 Cor. 3:10-15). Only through God's design will a church grow in a wholesome and rich way. All else falls short. That's why so many of the megachurches of the past are now empty shells with no life. Can we discern the sound of the trumpet? Are we going to build by God's standard and measure? Even the psalmist says,

Unless the LORD builds the house, its builders labor in vain. Unless the LORD watches over the city, the watchmen stand guard in vain (Ps. 127:1).

CHAPTER EIGHT

BOOT CAMPS OF GOD

TRAINING LEADERS IN LOVE AND UNITY

The Warrior took me back to see the small group again and I was amazed at what I saw! The young warriors were larger, more muscular and more fierce looking than the older warriors. In fact, each generation of warriors was more muscular and fierce then the generation before them.

I was about to ask how the warriors got so strong, but the Lord knew the question I was about to ask. He said, "Because each one works out harder in the house where he trains."

At this point I knew that the Warrior who had been showing me these things was indeed the Lord.

Pastor Dirk Lawyer of Resurrection Church in Portsmouth,

Ohio, has an interesting way of looking at this subject by utilizing types and shadows from the Old Testament. Pastor Dirk uses 1 Chronicles 20:6,7:

> In still another battle, which took place at Gath, there was a huge man with six fingers on each hand and six toes on each foot—twenty-four in all. He also was descended from Rapha. When he taunted Israel, Jonathan son of Shimea, David's brother, killed him.

Using this text as his illustration, Pastor Dirk likened the giant to young men being released prematurely into ministry:

> This is one of the giants...that steals the precious seed of the young men in ministry. Six speaks of the number of man, two speaks of the witness, the fingers speak of works; so, what we have is a witness of carnal works. How many know that when you loan yourself out prematurely, you're doing a lot of sweating? How many know that as a priest, you are not allowed to sweat? The giant has six toes; feet speak of walking, so it speaks of a witness of a carnal walk. A young man has each of these. If he is launched out prematurely, he will have a witness of carnal works and a carnal walk and that's all he'll ever produce.
>
> This giant had no name, because guess what name was on his head? Your name! He had no name; he was recognized by his six fingers and six toes. A young man in ministry that has no anointing and has gone on before God in his call, will always have no name in the eyes of God, but will always be recognized by his carnal walk and carnal works. Wood, hay, and stubble...we've just got

to let the fire burn it off.

Those who leave the house early and are not properly fathered and brought to that place of preparation have dominated the Christian scene in past decades. But God is raising up leaders who realize the mistakes of the past. Pastor John Diana said this about building:

> I've learned a lot about building by building improperly. There is nothing like making mistakes or making bad decisions, to help you make good decisions. For me, a crisis is a good motivation to do it right the next time. When you see something that you poured blood, sweat, and tears into, but you didn't do it right and you see it crumble because of the wind that comes, you don't want to go through that again. I'm not doing that again. I'm going to do it right the first time. This time it will be able to stand the winds of adversity.

DEVELOPING SONS FOR WARFARE

Every father should desire his son to go beyond him. This obviously was the case with the young warriors whom I saw in my vision. Pastor Thurlow Switzer, a translocal minister, has an interesting observation on this subject from the life of David. Switzer says:

> I am fascinated that when David killed Goliath, the first thing that happened up on the hill is that Saul turned to his associate and asked, "Find out who that man's father is!" (See 1 Sam. 17:55.)
>
> Whenever you see a son developing, or someone who

has come forth, the question should be, Who developed that person? When there are sons that are able to go into battle and have the courage to take on odds that no one else is willing to take and who are willing to be leaders, you want to find out who developed them. So the test of fruitfulness in your life is how many have you encouraged to take on odds and be courageous and able to overcome and affect ministry as a result of your life?

Pastor Ray Guinn adds:

The definition of church is the Greek word *ecclesia*, which means the "called out one." It comes from the Old Testament, when the trumpet was blown and the people were called out to assemble for the purpose of warfare, worship and hearing the Word taught. They are called out for a specific function. When Jesus talked about building the church in Matthew 16:18, He said, "I will build my church." In that context He is saying, I am calling people out; the trumpet is going to sound and they're being called out and assembled (I am going to build them), but I am going to send this group against the gates of hell (it's a military expression), and the gates of hell are not going to prevail.

If we don't have sons, the army can't draft them to do warfare. If we're not birthing any sons, there isn't going to be anyone to do the fighting. The reason is, we're doing the fighting among ourselves; we're killing each other. We've got to learn how to let this spiritual fathering bring some spiritual healing to the Church, so God can call these sons and send them out to do warfare.

Apostle Emanuele Cannistraci ministered at a conference for pastors in Indonesia. They came by boat – not luxury liners with modern conveniences, but dirty, old, crowded skiffs. It took five days of traveling time for many of them, but they came to be challenged and to have hands laid on them. The cry of their hearts, however, was to have a spiritual father. Hundreds of these humble men of God grabbed and pulled at Emanuele asking, "Please, be our father."

He sorrowfully replied, "I can't father this many people."

There is such hunger in the world today. There are leaders who realize they need to be fathered and are seeking men of God who can impart to them. These believers realize that it takes more than a name-it-and-claim-it belief, more than hyper-faith or other such short cuts. It takes honorable fathers imparting biblical principles that can weather any challenge in life.

THERE ARE LEADERS WHO REALIZE THEY NEED TO BE FATHERED AND THEY KNOW IT TAKES MORE THAN A NAME-IT-AND-CLAIM-IT BELIEF, MORE THAN HYPER-FAITH OR OTHER SHORT CUTS. WHAT IT TAKES IS HONORABLE FATHERS.

TRAINING IN THE HOUSE

The training ground for people called into ministry is the local church. Seminaries and Bible schools can supplement the local church, but they can't replace it as a training ground. Students who have spent years in Bible school come out confident, but soon find out that they are ill-prepared for ministry. Seminaries and Bible schools cannot prepare a pastor for ministry in the local church; only ministry in the local church can do that. The young warriors in my vision had been trained in the local church (the house) and their training had been complete and effective.

> It was he who gave some to be apostles, some to be prophets, some to be evangelists, and some to be pastors and teachers, to prepare God's people for works of service, so that the body of Christ may be built up (Eph. 4:11,12).

The only way this is accomplished is for the fivefold ministry to prepare God's people for works of service because God's desire is for His Body to be "built up." Many have built on the foundation of denominational supervisors, regional overseers, corporate types from XYZ Bible School or as independents, but it takes apostles, prophets, evangelists, pastors and teachers to father a strong generation that fights effectively for the Lord.

I think the reason the local church is no longer the accepted place for training believers for ministry is that most local churches are incapable of doing it and have no desire to do it. I believe the same is true of the school of the prophets. Training prophets should be a function of the local church, but we see ministries (parachurch groups) doing this, instead of the local church. This is one reason so many prophets don't know how to function in the context of the local church. There is no substitute for the local church as a training center.

HONOR THOSE OVER US

David Newell, who spent 24 years as copastor with Pastor

Charles Green in New Orleans and currently is planting a church in Cary, North Carolina, says, "I don't believe God will honor us by giving us authority unless we are willing to honor the senior man" (see 1 Tim. 5:17). There will never be effective training in the house unless we esteem the man over us. If we can't esteem him, we will never be esteemed.

The lessons we fail to learn in the "house" will come back repeatedly until we learn them. That is a biblical principle. In other words, what goes around comes around. Pastor Dave tells this story:

> We had a guy a number of years ago who was kind of sneaky. He would sneak up to people and say, "The pastor had a good word this morning. It was all right, but we're having a little home fellowship; would you like to join us? We are going to get into some really heavy revvy (revelation), some real meat of the Word. That was good milk we heard this morning, but we're going to get into some deep stuff."
>
> We began to hear about this matter; in fact two prophets picked out these people and said to watch them. Eventually Pastor Green said, "Hey Dave, come here. We've got to deal with this; we have to meet with this couple in my office." When we confronted the guy, he went ballistic—just totally ballistic, calling Pastor Green the Antichrist and some other names.
>
> Pastor Green, the master of understatement, said, "I discern you're not happy here."
>
> Pastor Green was also the master of greasing the skids. He said, "Why don't you find a place where you can be happy, so you can rejoice with them?"
>
> They left the church and a couple of years later, the

same fellow called pastor Green and said, "Brother Green, this is so-and-so, and I've called to ask you to forgive me for all the problems I caused you."

Pastor Green said, "You know I'll do that! I'll definitely forgive you, but can I ask you a question? Are you pastoring somewhere now?"

The man replied, "I'm not only pastoring, but there is someone in my church who is like me when I was in your church. When I went to God to remove the problem, your face came before me." God spoke to the man and said, "I won't deal with that problem until you go back and deal with the original problem."

Yes, what goes around comes around!

ATTACK SEPARATELY

The Lord said to me, "Are you ready to see the corporate anointing on the day of battle?"

I said, "Yes, Lord, I'm ready to see the corporate anointing on the day of battle!"

The trumpet sounded a long, loud call. All the troops moved out of their camps and went to the top of the hill. There they stopped.

The Lord said, "Look at them!"

I could see that each group carried a different banner and wore a different-colored uniform from other groups. The Army of God was once again preparing to attack the enemy.

The Lord said, "This group is going to attack them through faith. This group is going to attack them through discipline. This group is going to attack them through deliverance. This group will attack through personal ministry. That is the prophetic battalion. That is the evangelist."

Before taking me to see the corporate anointing on the day of battle, the Lord again showed me the group in this vision that had been so ineffective. It was the large group that had formed the circles and faced inward, spilling their seed on the ground.

The large group was now divided into smaller groups. These smaller groups were now all under their own banners and were going to attack the enemy with their own specialty: Those under the faith banner were going to attack through faith; those under the deliverance banner were going to attack through deliverance; those under the prophetic banner were going to attack through the prophetic, etc. The churches knew no other way but to attack through their specialty. They had to do it that way.

Pastor David Loveless of Discovery Church in Orlando, Florida, has tremendous insight into how this specialization between various groups separates us from seeing the larger picture. He says:

Years ago, I was jogging and the Lord brought to mind the passage in John 14:2 (*NASB*), that says, "In My Father's house [singular] there are many dwelling places [plural]." I just kept mulling and meditating on that passage and the Lord started showing me how there is supposed to be only one type of Church, although there are many expressions inside that church.

He gave me a picture of a literal house—the kind of

house you and I live in—with a number of rooms in the house, with each room having a different function: the living room has a function; the bedroom has a function; the kitchen has a function; the bathroom has a function; the garage has a function, etc.

The Lord seemed to say to me, "Within the Church there is supposed to be one entity, but inside there are a number of different rooms that are different expressions of Me." What people tend to do is build an entire house just based on one of those rooms.

This is exactly what I was seeing in the vision the Lord gave me: groups, denominations, churches, and networks that had built their ministries on one facet of the gospel. Pastor Loveless gives this humorous illustration of these churches:

REPEATING-SALVATION VERSION OF CHURCH

I worked for Barney's Barnacles. So as I'm working there at his store, Barney shares with me about the church he goes to and how it has been helpful to him. I ask him the name of the church and he tells me it's Main Street Temple. So I go to Main Street Temple and I hear the message of the gospel presented. After several weeks I see that's exactly what I need in my life. I invite Christ into my life and begin attending church there with my family. Two years later I'm still getting saved every week because I'm still hearing the gospel presented in the long-form version. Every Sunday people are invited to come down the aisle and invite Jesus into their lives—for the 40th time. After a couple of years I've been thoroughly saved, but something is going wrong in my life.

HEAVY-STUDY VERSION OF CHURCH

Then all of sudden I meet Henry, down at the racquetball club. Henry starts telling me about a church he goes to where he is being fed. The Word is enriching him. What I need is to be a part of a church like his where I can be fed. Salvation is not enough; you need to be taught. So I go down to the Teaching Center of Orlando and the first thing I notice when I drive up to the Teaching Center is that people are getting out of their vans and cars with briefcases. They have notebooks, rulers, study guides, markers and pens. In church everyone sits there taking notes; this is very serious stuff. During the first several months I get acquainted with the people in this church and I find out that these people have huge credit lines at Home Depot, Lowe's and Builders Square because they have to keep building book shelves. For the next couple of years I buy my markers, pens and rulers. I go to Home Depot and get three new bookshelves to put my new books on. Every Sunday I go to church and take notes and put them in my briefcase so I can take more notes. A couple of years later I feel fed, but you know what? Now there is something going on within my soul. I don't feel connected with God. In fact I never felt loved and touched by the experience of my Father.

CRY-MY-HEART VERSION OF CHURCH

So, down the street I meet Henrietta. She tells me about Worship Center of Orlando. She says, "You need to come down to Worship Center of Orlando. You'll be touched. Our worship is unbelievable." Therefore I go down to the Worship Center of Orlando. When I walk in I immediately see people on their knees, crying and singing.

I've never seen anything like this before, I do what I see
everybody else doing. I look for someone to work up a cry
with because I don't know how to cry. But after a couple
of weeks my heart starts getting really touched by the
intimate worship that is going on. For the next couple of
years I do that until can't cry anymore; I can't sway anymore and I'm getting too old to dance.

HEALING-POWER-OF-GOD VERSION OF CHURCH

All of a sudden I meet Gertrude and she tells me, "No,
no, no, that's not what you need; you need to come to
Billy Bob's Healing Center. That's what you really need."
I realize my diapers were too tight when I came out of
the womb and I need to be healed. I need to be physically
touched, so, I go to Billy Bob's Healing. When people are
touched they fall down like dominoes; I've never seen
anything like this in my life. I think this is what I need
so I let them take me through personal restoration and
I get personally restored...and I get personally restored...
and I get personally restored.... I keep going back to the
womb...back to the womb and I'm really getting reac-
quainted with my mother now. In a couple of years I've
been touched, I've been encouraged, but I don't want to
go back to the womb anymore. I want to grow up! I want
to get something done with my life!

Then all of a sudden I turn around and I meet some-
body else and on and on and on the story goes...

Barney's church, Henry's church, Henrietta's church and
Gertrude's church—all these churches were just like the churches
of the battalions that I saw in my vision. Their focus is in one
direction when the Bible teaches us to be good in all these things:

salvation, healing, prayer, evangelism, worship, servanthood, relationships, teaching, equipping, sending, etc. (see Rom. 12:9-18; 1
Tim. 4:7-16; 2 Tim. 4:2; 2 Pet. 1:5-7).

The battalions I saw were ineffective against the enemy.
Because they could only attack the enemy from one position,
they were limited to the thing they did well. They had no strategy against the enemy because of the churches' limitations. If
they were a faith church and their faith didn't bring victory, they
had no alternative. If the church was a teaching church and their
teaching alone couldn't bring victory, they had no alternative. If
their church is a deliverance church...if their church is a healing
church...and on and on it goes. God has called His Church to be
the total package with the total answer.

The foundation for proper building is found in "apostles
and prophets" as mentioned in Ephesians 2:20 with Jesus as the
Cornerstone. Many have built on the foundation of denominational supervisors, regional overseers, corporate types from XYZ
Bible School or as independents, but it takes the apostles and
prophets as fathers in Christ to raise up a strong generation that
fights effectively for the Lord.

YES, THERE IS A BATTLE

"There are a lot of churches that don't even believe they're in a
fight," says Bruce Gunkle. He explains:

> A lot of people don't believe the devil can do much to
> us if we're Christians. That's all part of what the devil
> does. The devil is at war with us. Many people have a
> non-aggression pact with the devil and they don't realize
> it. They've been taught that the devil can't touch them.
> They say, 'I'm not worried about it!' Meanwhile they're
> losing their family; they're losing their homes; they're

losing their jobs and they don't understand what's going on. They've been taught incorrectly; the devil is an expert at war and what's happening here is a scheme of his.

The enemy, you have to understand, is always plotting against us. We have a purpose that God has given us and the devil has an anti-purpose. What the Church doesn't understand is that the devil is not at war with Jesus because Jesus defeated the devil. The devil is at war with us! He wants to stop the Kingdom from coming in by defeating us because the devil knows that Jesus works through us. It's us he's after, not Jesus. Jesus already defeated him.

Revelation 19:19 says that we are "his army." An army is trained for a specific purpose, and that is to fight! We are not trained as the Army of God to go lie on the beach. We are in a real war against a real enemy.

CHAPTER NINE

THE
REMNANT
ARMY

GOD'S USE OF UNIFIED WARRIORS

The Lord said, "Let us go and inspect that small group."

I went with Him to see the small group. They were not in a group like the other battalions I had seen, but were arrayed in rows. Nor did they all wear the same uniform. In the first row there were men in the discipleship uniform, the holiness uniform, Pentecostal uniform, charismatic uniform, faith uniform—every kind of uniform you could imagine.

I said, "They look like a ragtag militia."

The Lord said, "These are My special troopers. They were seen as misfits when they were in the larger battalions. Their vision went beyond what My Church accepts as normal. They were misfits because they had something stirring within them; they could not tolerate standing *around in circles spilling their seed. Look at the uniforms of the troops behind them."*

When I looked beyond the first row, I could see that the remainder of the troops wore uniforms of many colors, much like the mental image I have always had of Joseph's coat of many colors. The collars of their uniforms were made up of every color. The soldiers represented every race, every ethnic group, every theological persuasion.

I asked, "Why have they stopped here?"

The Lord said, "Because they are surveying the battle-field."

The small group was surveying the battlefield and thinking about their plan. The first line was wearing traditional church uniforms that matched their banners: a Pentecostal uniform, a charismatic uniform, a faith uniform, a holiness uniform, etc. This was to lead the enemy to believe that it was business as usual and this was the same kind of Kingdom Army they had defeated so many times before. God's Army, in essence, were disguising themselves.

Behind the first line were more lines of warriors, but they were dressed differently. They had on what appeared to be Joseph's coat. The Army of God had one line wearing the coat of the traditional church, but every line behind them was wearing the coat that represented the approval and mantle of the Father.

EMBRACE ALL TRUTH

The Army of God was wearing a multicolored coat which represents all the moves of God from past to present and all the truths of God from past to present. In other words, they had gleaned all they could from all that was available. This is why, as I mentioned in chapter one, I like to refer to myself as being a Presbyterian because I believe in the plurality of elders; I'm Episcopalian because I believe in the authority of the bishops; I'm Methodist because I believe in small group dynamics; I'm Baptist because I believe in baptism by immersion; I'm Pentecostal because I believe in speaking in tongues; I'm Mennonite because I believe in the community life of the saints, etc.

In the same way, we need to embrace the various charismatic moves of the Spirit: word of faith, healing, deliverance, latter rain, manifest sons, revival and church restoration movements. We can take what others have learned before us and embrace it, throw out what we know to be wrong and put on a shelf the things that we currently aren't sure of for further consideration at a later date.

NO SUPERSTARS

For many years we've heard the present-day prophets speak of the end-time Army of God, and how they would "come out of hiddenness." There would be no superstars, but there would be a mighty army fighting together and effectively destroying the work of the enemy. They would build churches according to the biblical pattern and build for the next generation; they would lose their lives in Christ and put an end to the "my ministry" mind-set. This small group represents that group of warriors that is committed to the success of one another. They were assembled and wearing the mantle of the Father. They had a corporate strategy and were preparing to come on the scene and do battle.

A SMALL ARMY, WAITING AND SURVEYING THE BATTLEFIELD

While the small Army of God was quietly waiting, surveying the battlefield, the large battalion was moving in to attack. The large group had no corporate anointing and no strategy, but they moved forward toward the enemy camp.

From where the armies of hell were gathered for battle I could hear the fierce screaming of the demons. From among the Army of God a large battalion named Faith began approaching the armies of hell, but they turned back because they had no faith. They kept believing that the battlefield would change, but it did not. The armies of hell remained fierce and intimidating.

The Army of God launched an assault on the enemy camp while Faith trailed behind. The small group had yet to move. A great slaughter was taking place on the battlefield; the Army of God was being defeated by the enemy.

Then I saw the small group begin to form a wedge.

I watched as the large battalions attacked the enemy and were soundly defeated. They were full of bravado and faith while they were in their circles, but when they actually confronted the enemy, they failed miserably.

Meanwhile the small group was planning an attack, only their attack was in God's order and timing. They were an army resolute in purpose and focused on the victory ahead. Their unity was apparent for the world to see; they loved one another with a covenantal love. What the small group was about to do is something that all of Christianity has been waiting for since the time of Christ: They were forming a wedge that would destroy everything that exalts itself against the knowledge of God!

THE WEDGE

Then I saw the small group begin to form a wedge.
"What are they doing?" I asked.
The Lord said, "This is the wisdom that was given to Moses. Some have said it is an elitist principle, some call it hierarchy, but to form a wedge is a tactic of warfare. The captains over

thousands are going first, not last."

The captains were at the front of the wedge, and I could see that every generation behind formed a new wedge. (There were actually four wedges in all.) The battle raged with new intensity as the wedge entered the enemy camp. The second wedge was even more aggressive than the first. They were literally pushing the older warriors through the battlefield. The older warriors were strong enough to do the fighting, but the force of the ministers behind them was such that the first wedge was powerfully driven through the heart of the enemy's camp.

Finally they broke through and surrounded the entire enemy army. The Army of God began to slaughter them; blood was running in the field. Suddenly God's warriors, both old and young, began running to the field I had seen at the beginning of the vision — the field where there was smoke and fire.

The wedge, a classic military maneuver, is formed by troops driving into the center of the enemy stronghold. The flanks of the wedge then employ a circling tactic. The wedge has some distinct military advantages both in the natural and spiritual realm. It provides maximum protection to the front of the formation and is easier for the commanders to control. It is a formation committed to going forward, but it has minimal protection to the rear.

The armor of God in Ephesians 6:14-17 is strikingly similar in its design to push forward with minimal protection for the back part of the body. The Army of God is also similar in its commitment to making advances against the enemy. The strength of any tactical formation is the interlocking field of view and field of fire; this is based on assigned sectors of coverage for each element. One weak element can be disastrous.

In the vision, four wedges formed one large wedge. Behind the first one were three others. The four wedges formed a single wedge by having one wedge in the center of the leading wedge and the other two with their points at the rear points of the leading wedge.

This point of the wedge ripped into the enemy stronghold and every line of saints that followed made the path of destruction wider and deeper. When a huge gaping assault was made into the enemy camp, the Army of God flanked the enemy camp, completely surrounding them. No demon escaped this assault; they were totally surrounded and slaughtered on the battlefield.

Many times the enemy had defeated the Army of God on the battlefield, but now things were different. The Army of God sliced through the enemy ranks and slaughtered them all. The reason for this great victory is the exponential anointing that was present.

UNITY IS THE ONLY THING THAT CAN BRING EXPONENTIAL ANOINTING.

GOD'S ARMY NEEDS AN EXPONENTIAL ANOINTING

Minister Gary Kivelowitz spoke on the exponential anointing at our last men's conference, but he didn't have that topic until he prayed for something to speak on. That's when the Lord told him to speak on exponential anointing. He wasn't exactly sure what exponential meant so he called his son, Steve, who is a trained mathematician, and asked him. After Steve gave him a brief definition, Gary asked him for an example.

Steve told him, "Dad, if you take 20 to the second power that's 20 times 20, or 400. If you take 20 to the third power, it's 20 times 20 times 20, or 8,000. That's exponential! Twenty to the fourth power is 160,000, and 20 to the fifth power is 3.2 million."

UNITY KINDLES AN EXPONENTIAL ANOINTING

The power of the wedge was awesome because of the anointing that multiplied on the battlefield. There was an exponential anointing on the day of Pentecost when 120 believers were in the Upper Room and tongues of fire appeared (see Acts 2:1-4). Unity is the only thing that can bring an exponential anointing. It's true that God is restoring power, but the reason He is restoring power is because He is restoring unity. Once we have the unity, He will give the power and authority. The Church has been trying to grasp power before it has grasped unity, but it doesn't work that way. What did the 120 have on the day of Pentecost? They had unity! They were praying together. They were fasting together, they were living together, and they believed together (see Acts 2:38-42). They made a commitment not to depart until His Spirit came. It was in that unity that the power of God came.

We see the exponential power of unity in Deuteronomy 32:30: "How could one man chase a thousand, or two put ten thousand to flight?" This is the kind of power that I saw on the battlefield. The enemy was no match for the Army of God.

There will always be obstacles to unity; opposition from within is common wherever the gospel is preached. Opposition will come from people who are or who were part of our ministry.

Lucifer rebelled against the Father in heaven; Jesus had Judas on earth – at some time you will experience rebellion.

UNITY, NOT REBELLION

Tim Martin, senior pastor of New Life Christian Fellowship in Imlay City, Michigan, tells this story of people who rebelled against him while they were part of his ministry. The sad thing about this story is that it's not that uncommon. Any pastor can tell you stories very similar to this one that happened to pastor Tim.

There were some men who came in as assistant pastors, and at first Tim thought he had good relationships with these men. After some time Tim could see that these people didn't care about the Body because they had no team concept. What they really wanted was position and recognition to use as stepping stones for their own ministries. One fellow who started his own church actually called every member of Tim's church and told them, "Hey, we're down the road, why don't you come and join us?"

Tim cried out before the Lord, "God, what am I doing wrong? What did I do to create this monster? Help! What do I do?"

The problem here didn't arise because Tim did something wrong; these things just happen. It happened to the Father, it happened to Jesus and it will happen to us. I believe this kind of rebellion will disqualify the rebel from any kind of meaningful future ministry. God hates rebellion. I believe that the rebel will never lead men on the battlefield. A rebel is relegated to a lesser position than the one to which he was originally called.

WEDGE-FORMING STRATEGY FROM EXODUS

The wedge is a strategy that is found in its simplest form in Exodus 18:21. Jethro, Moses' father-in-law, gave this advice to Moses: "Select capable men from all the people—men who fear

God, trustworthy men who hate dishonest gain—and appoint them as officials over thousands, hundreds, fifties, and tens." The classic wedge strategy is to appoint "men who fear God, trustworthy men who hate dishonest gain," who would not withdraw from leading others into the heart of the battle.

The wedge formation comes from the time of Moses. This was no surprise to me because I knew the plan had been given to him. What surprised me was that Moses was in the wedge. Everything he did and taught in his lifetime made inroads into the enemy camp and made a path for others to follow. All the Old Testament men and women of God were in the wedge. What they did in their lifetimes was making a path for those behind them.

In the ranks that followed were the New Testament saints: Paul, Peter, Luke, John, Matthew, Barnabas, Timothy and others. They were all there, pushing forward with great joy in the time of battle. Although the ones identifiable were positioned in the front of the four wedges (that formed one wedge), the nameless saints in the back were the most powerful. These powerful saints were using what others did previously to force their way forward, pushing the saints in front of them.

Because of the tremendous momentum, there seemed to be no resistance from the enemy. The momentum came from the centuries of preparation of the wedge. The wedge began as a concept in the book of Exodus and it grew as the unity within the Kingdom grew. The wedge is still forming in this day and the strongest warriors are still to come. They will take their place in the back of the triangle and push those who have gone ahead through the enemy stronghold.

EVERY BATTLE HAS A DIFFERENT STRATEGY

Every battle that Israel fought in the Old Testament required a different strategy. Sometimes a battle required the blowing of horns and shouting as Gideon did; sometimes it required only a smooth stone such as David used. Sometimes a week-long march was necessary as in the case of Joshua at Jericho. Most of these battles obviously used the strategy employed by Moses— the wedge. A leader determines in his heart that he is going to advance the Kingdom in battle, does it, and consequently others follow in his path.

In the 1500s, Martin Luther realized that salvation was not by works, but rather by faith through God's grace. Faith and grace are not a revelation to the modern Christian. In fact most Christians probably learn about that on their first day as believers. However, to Martin Luther, this was a huge breakthrough. He was able to use this revelation to make vast breakthroughs into the enemy camp and many followed his example. Martin Luther became part of the wedge because of what he accomplished in his day.

CHAPTER TEN

IN THE
FRAY OF
BATTLE
STANDING FIRM IN GOD'S FAITHFULNESS

Suddenly the sky was filled with objects flying overhead. These things were coming from the houses that I had seen being built. I realized that these flying objects were in fact the prayers of the saints, who were doing spiritual warfare and tearing down powers and principalities.

Down on the field where there was fire and smoke, warriors who were evangelists went into the field. There they began reaching under the fire and smoke and pulling out golden souls. As they were doing this, baskets of golden souls began to form in the midst of the battlefield. A line of these baskets formed, leading all the way back to the houses which had been built.

Some men came running out from the midst of the battle.

At first I thought they were cowards, but the Lord said, "Those are My platoons of pastors going back to gather the harvest into My house and raise up generation after generation until I come."

The saints – young and old, male and female, black and white, brown and yellow – were sending up prayers. These prayers were so powerful that they could be felt like projectiles going overhead. The ministry of the prayer warrior had come to a place of maturity and had now formed its own wedge against the enemy.

Many unnoticed and unappreciated prayer warriors over the years were now rallying the troops in the house. There was an anointing for prayer in the houses and these people were seeking God as never before. The houses were full of all those who were not able to go into the field, but who felt the calling to kneel or lie prostrate in the houses and demolish the powers and principalities through prayer. Their prayers were accurate—they were not beating the air. They could zero in on the target with deadly precision. The enemy had no defense for this attack and was staggering under the onslaught.

Because of the prayers that were going up, the enemy had no way to resist the evangelists who could now go and harvest the souls in the fields and bring them into the house where they would be cared for. Great importance was placed on getting the souls back to the houses. As long as they were out of the houses, they were still in danger.

Under a barrage of fire and smoke, the warrior evangelists were reaching and pulling out souls. The gift of an evangelist is to reach into dark places where there is fire and smoke and from the darkness bring souls to Christ.

THE LATTER RAIN

Zechariah 10 indicates that the latter rain will be greater than the former rain. God spoke to me on this issue some time ago. He asked me, "What happens between the former and the latter rains? If there was a former rain—which means it came in the past—and the latter rain is the rain that is coming, what is going to happen between the two?"

The Lord showed me that between the former rain and the latter rain there is a vapor (condensation) that must come up from the earth and form clouds. Rain cannot come again until vapor from the earth has reached the clouds. The Lord revealed that the latter rain is a return of our prayers.

Acts 10:4 says that our prayers go up as a memorial offering before God. If we pray for revival, we will get revival; if we pray for healing, we will get healing. If we pray for others they will be blessed. Whatever we pray for will rise up like vapors into clouds and burst forth in rain. The latter rain is the sum total of prayer that has gone up from all the saints and is poured out upon the earth.

I asked God, "How does this relate to what we are doing?"

He said, "Revival won't come unless you pray for a storm, and that storm will be the latter rain."

There are three things that God wants to accomplish with the latter rain: (1) revival, (2) restoration and (3) reformation— that is, revival and restoration of the Church and reformation of cities and countries. But the reformation of cities and countries will not take place unless there has been revival in the Church and a restoration of the Church. Currently we are somewhere between the former rain and the latter rain. It is up to us to fill the clouds of heaven.

The Lord said one more thing to me. He said, "If Christianity is all about walking in My presence, why can't you find prayer in the average church budget? My House will be a house of prayer, but man has taken programs and put them in the place of prayer."

DOING THE WORK OF AN EVANGELIST

Any Christian bookstore will have a number of books on evangelism. Some evangelistic plans are very elaborate and some are very simple. Just because an evangelistic plan worked for another church, doesn't mean it will work for your church. Whatever the strategy, the plan will always depend on the basics. If a church won't pray for souls, it won't get any. It's that simple. Some of the most effective plans are the simplest if the church is willing to pray.

Pastor Scott Loughrige has a simple evangelistic plan that works. His church builds the Kingdom because they are willing to pray. He takes about three to five minutes on a Sunday morning and does a little teaching on evangelism. While Scott is speaking, he asks the congregation to take out paper and write down the names of people they want to see saved. The people write down names, and then he asks if there is anyone in church who was invited and is not saved. If there is a response, he asks them to write their names down. The congregation then comes into agreement by praying over the names, realizing that these people are going to be saved. Pastor Scott says:

> It's about time we begin to pray for our loved ones before it [salvation] ever happens, realizing that it is going to happen. We put just one name on that piece of paper and pray over it until the individual gets saved. We have a great time in the Lord, because we know that some of those people are going to be saved that week.

After they pray, Scott tells them it's not enough to just pray;

now they must call on them or invite them over to eat. This simple practice works! Sixty people have been saved in the last two months using this method. His emphasis is on giving the people some practical training and then walking them through it.

We don't have to be gifted evangelists, reaching into dark and dangerous places to rescue souls. We can all do the work of an evangelist, but it must always start with prayer.

THEY'RE NOT COWARDS

I should have known that those pastors were not running from the battle, because true pastors would never run from a battle—they would relish it. They were running to the thing that they love to do even more than going to battle. They were running to gather souls. Pastors love to gather, as a shepherd gathers sheep. They would begin to nurture and strengthen these new believers. All pastors want their children to become big and strong so that one day they can be part of God's wedge against the enemy. A true pastor would visualize his sons in the future, at his back, pushing him through the enemy's battlefield, destroying the enemy's strongholds.

PASTORS MUST BE MEN OF COURAGE. THEY MUST NOT GIVE IN TO POPULAR OPINION OR BE INFLUENCED BY THE BIG DONORS OF THE MINISTRY.

Pastors must be men of courage. They must not give in to popular opinion or be influenced by the big donors of the ministry. God wants a new kind of leader. He wants a leader who knows that his calling is not from a church board, but from Him. The pastor must know he is called to dwell in, dig a well in, build an altar in and prosper and grow a nation in the place where he pastors.

STAND FIRM

Years ago, the second church I pastored was a Baptist church that was filled with the Holy Ghost. The church had about 100 members when I got there and after about a year we had about 500. After my first year there the church board asked me to come to a meeting where they had intended to fire me!

They said, "We're firing you, Brother Kelly; we're stopping your pay as of tomorrow."

I said, "That's okay! That's fine."

"You're not upset?"

"No, I'm not upset."

The board members inquired, "What are you going to do?"

"I'm going to preach on Sunday morning."

"But we fired you!"

"Yes, I know. But God hired me and I'm going to stay until He tells me to go. My calling and anointing are for this place and I'm not leaving. Furthermore, I want all of you members of this board to leave."

The whole board left the church and the church grew and God blessed it. I had to make a decision; I wasn't going to allow a carnal, unbiblical church board to run me off from where God had placed me.

FOUNDATIONS APPEAR

Then I saw apostles and prophets in the harvest field, on the battlefield and back at the houses. The prophets were prophesying and the parts of the Body began coming together. The apostles were giving strategies and tactics. I could see a mighty fighting force being formed and taking shape under the guidance of the apostles. A harvest was taking place and, simultaneously, the harvest was being formed into a fighting force.

We all know what the pastor, evangelist and teacher do. Yet when it comes to the prophet and the apostle, there is confusion. Some would say that apostles and prophets are no longer in the Church because they are no longer needed. But Ephesians 4:13 says in reference to the members of the fivefold ministry that they will all be in the Church "until we all reach unity in the faith and in the knowledge of the Son of God and become mature, attaining to the whole measure of the fullness of Christ."

THREE CATEGORIES

In my vision I saw that there were three basic categories of apostles and prophets: those in the harvest field, those in the battlefield, and those in the house. In these three areas we will soon see great changes in the new millennium because of their strategy, wisdom and building skills. They will be used to bring unity to ministries that have been fragmented and in disarray.

When Jesus chose the original apostles, they were immature; they were not yet mature and seasoned. When prophets of the

Old Testament were called, they were often immature. It was over a period of time that they matured. What was happening in the '90s was that the apostle and prophet were coming of age, and because of their maturing, they are makeing a huge impact on the Body of Christ. Things will not remain the same in the Body of Christ! There will be great victory in the harvest field, the battlefield and in the house!

SHOW US!

Then everything stopped. Nothing else came to me in vision or dream. Then the Lord said to me, "I will not show you the rest because that is for no man to know. There are men in My ministry who want a guarantee of the end time. They want to know beforehand what is going to happen. Tell them it is a battle, but there is a corporate anointing for the battle."

The Lord showed me that the other group was also anointed—the group which had been so easily defeated by the enemy. "Theirs was an individual anointing," He said, "and it was every man for himself on the battlefield. Because these lacked the corporate anointing, when one warrior was attacked, there were no other warriors there to help him fend off the enemy. They were not fighting back-to-back!

"However, when one has the corporate anointing and the enemy attacks, it is like they are attacking all of My Army. Victory will not come through the ferocity of a single warrior, but through the ferocity of the brothers and sisters who join him in battle."

Deuteronomy 32:30,31 says, "How could one man chase a thousand, or two put ten thousand to flight, unless their Rock had sold them, unless the Lord had given them up? For their rock is not like our Rock, as even our enemies concede." There are three men in this passage: One man is standing alone and apart from two other men. The man who is alone is having some success, but he is only one fifth as successful as the two men who are together. Now if this one man were added to the other two, we would have the beginning of exponential anointing. In fact, the way God multiplies is even greater than the exponential mathematical equation because God says that one plus one equals 10,000.

ALIGN YOURSELF WITH OTHERS

Every Christian has an anointing and even when standing alone can have some success. But what the Spirit is saying to the Church today is to take your anointing and align yourself with like-minded brothers and sisters who want to build the Kingdom. By aligning yourself with others, you are then adding (a third, a fourth, a fifth, etc.) to the exponential equation.

We are living stones being built into a spiritual house (see 1 Pet. 2:5), and the apostle is the stone mason. The apostle will do as Nehemiah did when he restored Jerusalem (see Nehemiah). The stones that had fallen and were strewn about were once again used to build the wall. Pastor Joe Warner puts it this way:

Nehemiah knew the incredible value of the burnt stones; he used these stones to rebuild an entire city. He got them out of the dirt, dusted them off, cleaned them and put them back in the wall.

ABUSED AND REJECTED STONES

The apostle is the one who will take the stones that have been broken down, abused and rejected and put them back in the wall (see Neh. 2:17; 3:32). He will find these living stones in the harvest field, on the battlefield and in the house, and will place them where they can use their talent and gifting.

The vast majority of what Jesus taught about was restoration. There are many faithful ministers of the gospel who have been abused, abandoned and forgotten. They received this poor treatment from their denomination, their pastor, a colaborer or a friend.

Uriah, the husband of Bathsheba, was a loyal soldier in David's army. Yet he was intentionally abandoned on the front line of battle to be killed, and the man who intentionally abandoned Uriah was a man after God's own heart—David (see 2 Sam. 11:6-21). Like Uriah, many ministers have been placed on the front lines of the battle and abandoned. They have been placed there, in many cases, by the well-intentioned, but they are left there with no support (financial, prayer, oversight, training, colaborers). The enemy easily picks them off because all their support has withdrawn, as in the case of Uriah.

A CONFIRMATION

Pastor Dion Boffo at our Men in Ministry Conference gave a powerful confirmation to my dreams and visions. During the praise and worship just prior to my sharing about the mighty Warrior and the Army of God, Pastor Boffo shared the following about his own vision:

> I saw, in the spirit, a great battle taking place. On the battlefield I saw hand-to-hand combat. I saw the Armies of God in disarray. I heard men crying out, "Where's the ark? We can't win without the ark!" Many men were fighting valiantly but could not prevail. They were waiting for an ark that was not coming. I then saw the men

who were sent to get the ark. They were trying to carry the ark amid the frenzy. They were trying to fight the enemy and grab the ark at the same time. They were in a rush to get it back. They kept dropping it and picking it up but it toppled over and the contents spilled out. The way they were picking it up and trying to carry it back was really a shame. My spirit was grieved.

I saw apostle Kelly, apostle Cannistraci and others gathered together in what looked like some kind of bunker or building. They were strategizing and planning. Occasionally a bomb would come over and explode. Apostle Kelly would duck his head, dirt would fall from the ceiling and he would continue. He looked somewhat annoyed that the bombs were coming in.

Suddenly I heard a voice thunder, "John, get up! Send your men! Go and get the ark!" Kelly stood up immediately and was somewhat puzzled, as if someone else was supposed to have done that already. As Kelly stood there God spoke again: "Go and send them, now!"

I then saw a group of mighty men (for lack of a better term). They were powerful men who walked together. They did not speak, but protected each other as they went. They seemed unaffected by the battle raging around them. They walked right through the frenzy. They flung the enemy like rag dolls and pushed through their own friendly forces. What is interesting is that they moved forward together with a purpose: to get the ark. They destroyed anything that got in their way. With the swipe of a hand or with a kick, they parted the enemy. They did not intend to engage the enemy unless their defined objective was threatened.

When the men arrived at the ark, they did not speak. Everyone backed away. They picked up the contents and placed them back in the ark. They all maintained their positions. Some gathered the things while others appeared to be standing reverently at guard positions. There was a great sense of respect all around. With precision they righted the ark, picked it up and began to carry it back. This whole process was accomplished with reverence and a worshipful attitude.

That was the end of Pastor Boffo's vision.

Pastor Boffo interprets his vision this way:

1. There was an awareness that what was lacking was the presence of the Lord.
2. It appeared that the first group who were sent to get the ark were well intentioned, but totally untrained, undisciplined, and lacking in strength, reverence, wisdom and perspective. Whoever trained them, didn't.
3. Because of the lack of training, there was a total lack of respect for the things of God—namely the things in the ark as well as for the ark itself. In their minds, the presence of God was in a thing rather than in a reality of being. The three things in the ark represent the priesthood of God (the rod which budded), the provision of God (the manna), and the precepts of God (the Ten Commandments). Because of the lack of respect (taking for granted the works of the Lord, i.e., sin) His presence was not there.
4. The second group of men who were sent were very strong individually and corporately. They were rooted, grounded, godly, secure and able to keep rank; they

understood their determined purpose and were not distracted from their objective.

5. Finally, those who will prevail in the battle must be men under authority. They must be righteous and holy— well prepared and exercised in godliness. As for Apostle Kelly, I believe God is encouraging him in the vision to send forth faithful men who will carry the presence of God into battle and turn the tide in the final push for world evangelism.

WARFARE

There are several ways to look at spiritual warfare: First is the spiritual point of view, where all that has to be done is to pray and tear down the forces of evil in heavenly places and continue to do this until Jesus comes. Second is the point of view that everything is predestined and nothing has to be done because the righteous will inherit the earth no matter what they do or don't do. I think both views have some merit; there is a lot that can be said for viewing spiritual warfare in each way.

What I see as God's plan is for the Body of Christ to replace all darkness with His kingdom, to take dominion in every realm of activity on earth, and to replace the kingdom of darkness with God's kingdom in economic, political, judicial and educational realms.

ADAM AND EVE FAILED

When God created Adam and Eve, He put them in a garden paradise. He then gave them authority and commanded them to be fruitful and multiply and subdue the earth (see Gen. 1:27-30). In other words, they were to expand the garden, but they failed.

With the first coming of Jesus, man was given another chance to take dominion over the earth. I believe God has called us to take over the planet. He's given us the authority over every power and principality, but it's not just taking authority over every demon, it's taking authority over everything in every realm. He is Lord of all, and if He is in us, He will rule over every realm through us—over the economic, political, judicial and educational realms.

LIMITATIONS CAN'T LIMIT US

We all have limitations. If your IQ is 190, it's not 191. If you have a doctorate, you probably don't have two. If you have four years of experience in your field, you don't have five. We are all limited—everyone of us, but with the wisdom of God, the knowledge of God, and the impartation of God's mind within us, we can do all things (see Phil. 4:13).

The Church is a Church of infinite power. God has called you to be a success right where you are. You're not a second-class minister in the kingdom of God! You're a first-class minister of the kingdom of God—His champion—sharing His grace, wisdom, power and strength with everyone you meet.

If you work in construction, be God's first-class minister on the construction site; if you teach, be God's first-class minister in the classroom. If you're a salesperson, be God's first-class minister in your outside selling or over the phone. Be God's kingdom builder!

If you're in school, don't say, "I'm only a student." You may say that outwardly to the ungodly, but to the godly you're a minister serving God in that school as a student. That is your mission field. That's where God is going to use you – not only to bring in the lost but to take charge of your surroundings. Right where you have been placed is where you begin to build the Kingdom. The Scriptures say:

How could one man chase a thousand, or two put ten thousand to flight, unless their Rock had sold them, unless the Lord had given them up? For their rock is not like our Rock, as even our enemies concede (Deut. 32:30,31).

God is with us. Now is the time to be bold, faithful and true in the fray of the battle. Individually and corporately, God wants us to be His kingdom builders, His champions, His end-time warriors.

JOHN P. KELLY

Over thirty years ago, John P. Kelly had a dramatic encounter with the power of Jesus Christ which radically altered his life. John's life to that point was a wide variety of experiences in education, business and sports into which God deposited a unique combination of gifts. From establishing the largest prison ministry in New Jersey, to spearheading apostolic ministry worldwide, John has forged paths for others to follow, influenced the lives of countless thousands and transformed many into vibrant leaders.

As a global apostolic strategist, Apostle Kelly has a three-fold calling: to be a voice concerning the apostolic movement, to mentor emerging apostles, and to give counsel to apostles in transition. To advance this calling he founded LEAD (Leadership Education for Apostolic Development) as a serving ministry to help men and women achieve their apostolic destinies. Apostle Kelly collaborates with and assists apostles in building and/or strengthening their apostolic networks through private consultations, seminars and institutes.

Apostle Kelly is one of the founders of the International Coalition of Apostles (ICA) and serves its presiding apostle Dr. C. Peter Wagner. As the Ambassador Apostle for ICA, John travels worldwide to assist in the development of emerging and established apostolic ministries and networks as well as convening numerous ICA Regional Summits throughout the United States.

He is the Chancellor of Kingdom Embassy University, a faculty member with Wagner Leadership Institute, a member of the Beacon College Board of Regents and an advisor on the boards of Global Compassion Network, American Action Coalition, and Hamilton Apostolic Council.

His background in business and education in economics has enabled him to be a force in the "transference of wealth movement." To advance the knowledge and equipping needed, LEAD conducts the annual Power to Get Wealth! Christian Wealth Builders Conference during the month of October each year in Dallas, Texas.

For more information, product information or to schedule speaking engagements, you can contact LEAD and Apostle John P. Kelly at

LEAD
PO Box 820067
Fort Worth, TX 76180
www.leadtoachieve.com
email: info@leadtoachieve.com

PAUL COSTA

D r. Paul Costa has been in the ministry for 27 years. Sixteen of those years he pastored churches, and the last 11 years he has ministered world-wide. Paul holds a B.A. from the University of Notre Dame and an M.A. and Ph.D. from the California Graduate School of Theology.

Besides having a strong pulpit ministry, Paul has a strong prophetic ministry to individuals and churches. He travels widely, prophetically releasing the saints of God into functional ministry. Paul is passionate about raising up leaders to fulfill their calling and to impact the world around them. He is also highly anointed with the gift of healing; numerous testimonies of dramatic healings have resulted from those touched by God through Paul's ministry.

Paul went to Notre Dame on a football scholarship, and played professional football for 10 years: 8 years with the Buffalo Bills (playing in 2 pro bowls) and 2 years in the now defunct World Football League.

Paul has been a guest on the 700 Club, TBN, PTL, and various other Christian TV and radio venues. He was the editor of The Networker, a cutting-edge apostolic/prophetic magazine for Christian leaders, and has co-authored several books with John Kelly. Paul teaches a course on Practical Apostolic Ministry, and has had various articles published, including an article in Ministries Today titled "Healthy Church Apostles." Paul is a member of the International Coalition of Apostles (ICA).

Paul has also owned and managed several businesses and teaches on marketplace ministry. Paul and Jan, his wife of 29 years, have one son, Clark, who is also in marketplace ministry.

For more information, product information or to schedule speaking engagements, you can contact Apostle Paul Costa at:

Paul Costa Ministry
www.paulcostaministry.org
Office: 817 788-8091
Mobile: 817 937-4185

RESOURCES

There are many great resources available through our website:

www.leadtoachieve.com

Look for these dynamic tools from Apostle John Kelly.

IMPLEMENTING APOSTOLIC MINISTRY - AM 101

This is a training course designed to increase your understanding regarding the Apostolic. The series is over eleven hours of comprehensive instruction by Dr. John P. Kelly that comes with a workbook and is designed to train and instruct leaders in the function of Apostolic Ministry. Available in both CD and DVD formats, it is a must for churches, leaders and ministries who are emerging and embracing an apostolic paradigm.

MASTER BUILDERS TRAINING INSTITUTES LEAD AND DR. JOHN P. KELLY

Net Menders & Tenders
The Craftsmanship of Building An Apostolic Network

This Institute is an intensive, practical, hands-on, "how-to-do-it" training experience dedicated to unlocking the apostolic revelation of networking. This course reveals an apostolic strategy to fulfill the Great Commission. It is designed to instruct the five-fold ministries in the art of networking to achieve strategic Kingdom expansion and explosive church growth. You can expect to understand The Types of Apostolic Networks, The Work of the Apostolic Anointing, Types and Methods of Authority, Structural and Governmental Alignment, How to Finance an Apostolic Network and the vital component of Apostolic Administration.

This Institute is eight sessions on CD and also comes with a course workbook.

Taking It On The Road
Developing A Financial Base & Building An Itinerate Ministry

This Institute is truly the first of its kind! It is comprised of nine sessions dedicated to the specific needs and responsibilities encountered by those in traveling ministry. This Institute deals with practical topics of vital importance such as Financing a Traveling Ministry, Proper Spiritual Covering, Networking, When & Where to Preach It and How To Receive an Offering. In addition, two session are dedicated to proper Administration that will protect your ministry, maximize your resources and help build your ministry and increase your effectiveness. You will learn how to produce a newsletter that impacts your audience and will generate support. Learn the value of offering media through your ministry and so much more!

Stones & Mortar
Building Apostolic Churches By Apostolic Methods

Learn the basics of building a strong, vibrant, spirit-led, apostolic/prophetic church. You will set the right foundation with Administration, understand The Mission Mirror, Preaching with Purpose to Build, Dispensations of Times and Seasons, going from a Pond to a Lake, utilizing The Secret Weapon of Dynamic Church Growth, how to Become a Developer, how to Build a Giving Church and the Benefits of an Apostolic Network. This Institute will help you break through the barriers and develop a thriving, growing, dynamic church body.

Women Arise!
God's Secret Weapon

All over the earth, women are being raised up! Long valued for their nurture and sensitivity to the Spirit, women have been overlooked for their strength, discernment, ability to wage war and hold places of authority. This audio message on CD will encourage and inspire women to embrace all God has for them and be released from bondages that have held them captive in the Church. A new paradigm opens as we recognize God's true order, and men and women see themselves as God designed them to be. Don't miss the opportunity to be impacted by this powerful message!

Look for these resources provided by Dr. Paul Costa also available on our website:**www.leadtoachieve.org**

Releasing The Ministry Of The Saints
Dr. Paul Costa - 3 Disc Series

There is a mighty move of God sweeping across the earth, shaking the foundations in preparation for the coming of the Lord. This move is The Ministry of The Saints. Its purpose is for God's people to carry out His will with effective strategy and force. We were created to subdue the earth with the radiating love of God that will transform all of society.

In this three part series, Paul will challenge you to release this powerful movement in your own life and propel you into greater things.

Healing Emotional Wounds and Scars
Dr. Paul Costa

Most people suffer from some kind of emotional pain at some point in their lives. They often find it easier to deal with physical ailments than emotional ailments, but if someone is suffering from an emotional wound, scar, or bruise, it is important to move on from being a victim.

In this booklet, Dr. Paul Costa explores the journey to complete healing of emotional wounds and scars. His insights will not only help you overcome your pain, but help equip you to reach out and bring healing to others.

End Time Warfare
Dr. Paul Costa

David had just defeated Goliath on the field of battle and was holding Goliath's head when Jonathan saw him and became one in spirit with David (1 Samuel 18:1). They were two warriors who immediately identified with one another and made covenant for the purpose of warfare.

To be in covenant with others in the body of Christ is for the purpose of warfare – that we might fill the earth with the glory of God. The enemy will resist us in every way possible; therefore, we must be in a strong place of covenant to war against the enemy effectively.

A covenantal mindset is visionary; it sees beyond our personal needs, to a place of caring for the Body of Christ. It sees the big picture from God's perspective.

Dive into this study and gain the insights Paul brings to the purpose of covenant and agape love in the strategy for End Time Warfare.

Key To The Anointing
Dr. Paul Costa

In order for Christians to be effective in ministry, they must be anointed by the Holy Spirit. In simple terms, the "anointing" is when the Holy Spirit is present to carry out some ministry or function through the believer. When the Holy Spirit ministers through the believer, there is success beyond our natural ability.

The desire of every Christian is to minister under the anointing so that we might bear fruit. But how do we walk in this outpouring of anointing? Can the anointing be increased in our lives?

In this booklet, Dr. Paul Costa shares with you the fundamental Key to the Anointing.

Conferences, Institutes & Opportunities

LEAD (Leadership Education for Apostolic Development) is dedicated to helping you achieve success! Throughout the year, LEAD sponsors many venues for training, encouragement and enrichment in specific areas.

For current information about upcoming opportunities, we encourage you to bookmark our website, www.leadtoachieve.com and to visit the site often. It is our desire to help you accomplish your mandate, propel you towards your vision and fulfill your destiny. It is this commitment to your success that drives us to provide continuous venues for men and women of God to receive instruction and impartation as well as have opportunities to meet one another and increase their sphere of influence and level of impact.

Power To Get Wealth!
Christian WealthBuilders Conference
Deuteronomy 8:18

This conference is held in Dallas, Texas, in October of each year. LEAD gathers some of the top Christian businessmen and women together to motivate you and offer practical instruction in wealth aquisition, wealth building and wealth distribution. Advancing the Kingdom of God on earth requires significant resources. God's people need control of these resources in order to direct the flow for maximum impact! Go to www.leadtoachieve.com and learn how YOU can be part of this "Transference of Wealth" movement!

Institute for Christian WealthBuilders
Deuteronomy 8:18

This Institute is a division of the International Christian WealthBuilders Foundation. It's mission and vision is based upon Deuteronomy 8:18, "And you shall remember the Lord your God, for it is He who gives you the **POWER TO GET WEALTH** that He may establish His covenant which He swore to your fathers as it is this day." The Foundation is committed to raising up Christian WealthBuilders to become wealth generators in order to be wealth distributors. The purpose of the Institute is to educate current and future wealth builders.

For more information and for student enrollment, go online to www.leadtoachieve.com and look for the link to WealthBuilders.

Look for these titles coming soon!

Act Like A Man
Dr. John P. Kelly with Dr. Paul Costa

This book was written by men to men! (Women should exercise caution when reading.) Too long our culture has attacked manhood and tried to "gender-blend" until masculinity has become synonymous with "biggot," "brute," and "neanderthal." It is time for men to be men again. This book will release you from false femininity and allow you to embrace your manhood with dignity, grace and purpose -- a must read!

APOSTOLICITY
"being apostolic without being an apostle..."
Dr. John P. Kelly with Dr. Philip R. Byler

Few are called to be pastors, full time missionaries or vocational church leaders. Fewer still are called to be contemporary apostles, yet, all are called to be effective as ministers of God's love and grace. APOSTOLICITY is a book about the Kingdom of God. It is about functioning within the opportunities of apostolic life -- managing earth's resources from heaven's point of view. With explanations of how an apostolic expression of church life works, it provides believers with a basic understanding of Kingdom experience, spiritual warfare and embracing one's vocation as a calling from God.